The Texas Overland
Expedition of 1863

CIVIL WAR CAMPAIGNS AND COMMANDERS SERIES

Under the General Editorship of Grady McWhiney

PUBLISHED

Battle in the Wilderness: Grant Meets Lee by Grady McWhiney
Death in September: The Antietam Campaign
        by Perry D. Jamieson
Texans in the Confederate Cavalry by Anne J. Bailey
Sam Bell Maxey and the Confederate Indians by John C. Waugh
The Saltville Massacre by Thomas D. Mays
General James Longstreet in the West: A Monumental Failure
        by Judith Lee Hallock
The Battle of the Crater by Jeff Kinard
*Cottonclads! The Battle of Galveston and the Defense of the
        Texas Coast* by Donald S. Frazier
A Deep Steady Thunder: The Battle of Chickamauga
        by Steven E. Woodworth
The Texas Overland Expedition of 1863 by Richard Lowe
Raphael Semmes and the Alabama by Spencer C. Tucker

The Texas Overland Expedition of 1863

WITHDRAWN

Richard Lowe

Under the General Editorship of Grady McWhiney

McWhiney
Foundation
Press

McMurry University
Abilene, Texas

Cataloging-in-Publication Data

Lowe, Richard G., 1942—
    The Texas overland expedition of 1863 / Richard Lowe; under the general editorship of Grady McWhiney.
        p. cm. — (Civil War campaigns and commanders)
        Includes bibliographical references and index.
        ISBN 1-886661-12-X (pbk)

    1. Louisiana—History—Civil War, 1861–1865—Campaigns. 2. Texas—History—Civil War, 1861–1865—Campaigns. 3. United States—History—Civil War, 1861–1865—Campaigns. I. McWhiney, Grady. II. Title. III. Series.
        E476.4.L64 1996
        973.7'37—dc20   95–51437
                                                                                        CIP

Copyright©1998, McWHINEY FOUNDATION PRESS

McMurry Station, Box 637
Abilene, TX 79697-0637

Printed in the United States of America

ISBN 1-886661-12-X

10 9 8 7 6 5 4 3 2 1

Book Designed by Rosenbohm Design Group

All inquiries regarding volume purchases of this book should be addressed to McWHINEY FOUNDATION PRESS, McMurry Station, Box 637, Abilene, TX 79697-0637. Telephone inquiries may be made by calling (915) 691-6681.

A Note on the Series

Few segments of America's past excite more interest than
Civil War battles and leaders. This ongoing series of brief,
lively, and authoritative books–*Civil War Campaigns and
Commanders*–salutes this passion with inexpensive and
accurate accounts that are readable in a sitting. Each volume,
separate and complete in itself, nevertheless conveys the
agony, glory, death, and wreckage that defined America's
greatest tragedy.

In this series, designed for Civil War enthusiasts as well as
the newly recruited, emphasis is on telling good stories.
Photographs and biographical sketches enhance the narrative
of each book, and maps depict events as they happened. Sound
history is meshed with the dramatic in a format that is just
lengthy enough to inform and yet satisfy.

Grady McWhiney
General Editor

CONTENTS

1. Cotton and Slaves   13

2. Into the Bayou Country   25

3. On to Texas   36

4. The Invasion Stalls   49

5. The Confederates Stalk   63

6. The Battle of Bayou Bourbeau   80

7. The Aftermath   101

Appendix A. Organization of Federal Forces   112

Appendix B. Organization of Confederate Forces   117

Further Reading   119

Index   124

The brief biographies accompanying the photographs were written by Grady McWhiney and David Coffey.

CAMPAIGNS AND COMMANDERS SERIES

Map Key

Geography

 Trees

 Marsh

 Fields

 Strategic Elevations

 Rivers

 Tactical Elevations

 Fords

 Orchards

 Political Boundaries

Human Construction

 Bridges

Railroads

Tactical Towns

● ○ Strategic Towns

□ ■ Buildings

† Church

Roads

Military

 Union Infantry

 Confederate Infantry

 Cavalry

ılı Artillery

 Headquarters

 Encampments

 Fortifications

Permanant Works

Hasty Works

 Obstructions

 Engagements

 Warships

 Gunboats

 Casemate Ironclad

Monitor

 Tactical Movements

 Strategic Movements

Maps by
Donald S. Frazier, Ph.D.
Abilene, Texas

MAPS

Routes to Texas   21

Invasion Route: Brashear City to Vermilionville   37

Invasion Route: Vermilionville to Opelousas   51

Buzzard's Prairie   52

Bayou Bourbeau: Situation at Noon   81

Bayou Bourbeau: End of Battle   97

Retreat: Bayou Bourbeau to New Iberia   106

PHOTOGRAPHS AND ILLUSTRATIONS

Andrew Jackson Hamilton	16
Nathaniel P. Banks	18
William B. Franklin	23
Richard Taylor	27
John G. Walker	28
Cadwallader C. Washburn	30
Albert L. Lee	32
Edmund J. Davis	33
Engagement with a Rebel Alligator	42-43
Edmund Kirby Smith	44
Federals crossing Vermilion Bayou	46
Thomas Green	50
Battle of Buzzard's Prairie	54-55
Stephen G. Burbridge	67
Oran M. Roberts	69
St. Landry Catholic Church	70-71
James P. Major	76
Arthur P. Bagby	77
Richard Coke	84
Attack on the 60th Indiana	86-87
Capture of the 67th Indiana	90-91
William Marland	94
William Marland at the bridge	95
James R. Slack	98
Opelousas Courthouse	102

The Texas Overland
Expedition of 1863

1
Cotton and Slaves

Spanish moss sways softly from the branches of oak and hickory trees along the banks of Bayou Bourbeau in south-central Louisiana, and the sounds of birds and small animals rustling through the undergrowth are only occasionally joined by the noise of a passing car on a nearby country lane. The unwary visitor might conclude that nothing of much importance ever happened here. It is so quiet. So isolated. And so peaceful. No historical markers or monuments reveal the secrets of this place, and even many of the residents in the surrounding countryside are unaware of what happened 130 years ago in the farm fields and woods bordering the bayou. But if they had walked along that narrow stream in the fall of 1863, along the same shady lanes and fence rows that were there when their Cajun ancestors lived nearby, they would have seen the blood and lightning of war. Where farmers bounce along on tractors and where yellow school buses meander along winding country roads today, men from Indiana and Ohio and Wisconsin and Texas slashed and tore at each other in the smoke and noise of battle those many years ago.

How the armies of Abraham Lincoln and Jefferson Davis even came to this isolated spot is an interesting story in itself. Ironically, it is a story that originally had nothing to do with Louisiana or the Cajun prairies bordering Bayou Bourbeau. The tale begins as early as the 1840s. When Louisiana's western neighbor, Texas, was joined to the United States in 1845, some Americans of the Northeastern states saw both promise and threat in the new territory. The rich soils and mild climate of eastern and central Texas promised prosperity for those who would settle and work the land. But Texas also threatened to extend and strengthen the hold of slavery on the western edge of the United States.

Some abolitionists and antislavery businessmen of New England determined to take advantage of the promise and eliminate the threat by settling Texas with solid Northern stock, families from the Northeastern and Midwestern states who would bring their free-labor agriculture to the new land, raise cotton for Northern textile mills, and save Texas for freedom. More efficient and more profitable free-labor farming would drive out the wasteful agriculture of bondage, and Texas would become a western buffer against the further extension of slavery. At least, that was the plan.

Not much more than talk was done to bring the plan to fruition before the Civil War, however. Textile mill owners and antislavery writers penned letters and pamphlets outlining the proposal, and some of them even urged Washington politicians to help the project along, but other events of the 1840s and 1850s distracted the nation from the plan to save Texas. The sectional dispute over California and the Southwest, the border war in Kansas, the Supreme Court's controversial decision in the case of the slave Dred Scott, John Brown's raid into Harpers Ferry—all diverted the country's eyes away from the fields and river valleys of Texas. Southern-born farmers settled there, planted thousands of acres of cotton—using slave labor—and enjoyed the prosperity that Texas had always promised. By the time Abraham Lincoln was nominated for the presidency in 1860, Texas had been lost by the North to slave-labor agriculture and Southern-oriented politics. If anyone doubted that, he had only to watch the Lone Star State fly to the colors of the new Confederate States of America in early 1861. Texans by the tens of thousands rushed to join dozens of new regiments forming to "turn back the Yankee hordes" and "save Texas from the Northern vandals." The chances of saving Texas for freedom now seemed altogether hopeless to most Northerners.

But others, including some of the same men who had urged the project from the beginning, saw the coming war as a perfect opportunity to accomplish what they had long desired—a takeover of Texas by the forces of freedom and the establishment of a stable supply of cotton for northeastern textile mills. Now, they reasoned, it would be easier than ever to get control of Texas. Now, they could ride into the Lone Star State under the Star-Spangled Banner and at the head of long blue columns of Federal troops, who would provide protection for Northern settlers and textile mill agents. It seemed that the Southern-born Texans had played right into their hands—if, that is, the Northerners could convince President Lincoln and the War Department to take advantage of the opportunity and grab Texas for the Union.

As early as 1861, the first year of the Civil War, Edward Atkinson, a powerful Massachusetts textile mill owner, suggested a free-labor invasion of Texas. In the spring of 1862 he traveled to Washington to lobby for a Federal military expedition to plant the flag on Texas soil. Atkinson's idea was seconded by some of the most powerful and prominent men in the North—Postmaster General Montgomery Blair, Massachusetts Governor John A. Andrew, Massachusetts politician and newly minted General Benjamin F. Butler, and the general in chief of all Federal armies, George B. McClellan. The political pressure to invade Texas increased in the summer and fall of 1862 when wartime cotton shortages forced many New England textile mills to shut down their clacking machinery, lock their gates, and send their workers home without pay. Now the powerful

Andrew Jackson Hamilton: born Alabama 1815; read law and was admitted to the bar in 1841; moved to Fayette County, Texas, in 1846, and three years later became state attorney general; member of the state legislature from 1851 to 1853; in 1859 elected to Congress "as an uncompromising Unionist, although speaking out for conciliation of the South"; Hamilton, who remained in Congress after other Texas representatives withdrew, returned to Texas in March 1861 and was again elected to the legislature as an opponent of seces- sion; regarded as a traitor after the war began, he fled in 1862 to Mexico and thence to Washington, D.C., where President Lincoln appointed him a brigadier general of volunteers and military gover- nor of Texas; Hamilton spent most of the remainder of the war in New Orleans; a controversial figure, whom Gideon Welles described as a "deceptive, vain, self-conceited partisan," his first appointment as brigadier general was never acted upon by the Senate and expired on March 4, 1863; Lincoln reappointed him to rank from September 18 and his appointment as governor was ratified by President Andrew Johnson in June 1865, where- upon Hamilton resigned his military commission; "tact, courage, efficiency, and moderation" charac- terized his fourteen months of service as governor until replaced in August 1866 by a regularly elected set of officials; he then became a member of the state supreme court where his decisions reflected a con- servative view; in 1868 he opposed the disfranchisement of southern whites; nom- inated for governor by the conservatives in 1869, he lost the election; his last polit- ical campaign occurred in 1873 when he attempted to challenge in court the elec- tion of the Democrats, who had ousted the Republicans; Hamilton died in 1875 in Austin, and was buried in Oakwood Cemetery.

New York Times, Secretary of State William Seward, Secretary of the Treasury Salmon P. Chase, and New York businessmen joined the crusade to reclaim Texas.

They found willing allies among refugee Texas Unionists who had fled their homes for the North rather than endure the persecution of their Confederate neighbors. Andrew Jackson Hamilton, the most prominent among them, was an Alabama native who had moved to Texas in 1846. Hamilton was an accomplished politician who had served as the state's attorney general, as a state legislator, and as a U.S. congressman. His refusal to bow under the pressure of the secessionists kept him in the U.S. Congress for months after other Texans had resigned and returned home to join the Southern war effort. When he finally did go home to the state capital of Austin in 1861, he was denounced as a traitor by many of his neighbors. Suspected by some fellow Texans of planning to overthrow the Confederate state government in Austin, he was forced to abandon his home and flee to nearby Mexico to save himself in 1862. Later that year he and other Texas Unionists banded together with Northeastern capitalists and antislavery politicians to prowl the corridors of the Capitol in Washington, pleading for a Federal invading army to save their state from the secessionists.

The dreams of the New Englanders and the desperate petitions of the Texas Unionists seemed to bear fruit in the fall of 1862. Hamilton was given a commission as a brigadier general of volunteers in the U.S. Army and appointed military governor of Texas. President Lincoln and Secretary of War Edwin Stanton even organized an expedition in September, to be led by Major General Nathaniel P. Banks, to invade the Lone Star State. But before the invasion could begin, General Banks was given command of the Federal Department of the Gulf, with instructions to focus on the defense of New Orleans and the conquest of the Mississippi River valley. Texas would have to wait.

Nathaniel P. Banks: born Massachusetts 1816; received little formal education; admitted to the bar in 1829; entered Massachusetts legislature, rising to speaker of the house; presided over the state's 1853 Constitutional Convention and was elected to the U.S. House of Representatives that same year; speaker of the House 1856; elected governor of Massachusetts in 1858, serving until 1861; at the outbreak of the Civil War, he offered his services to the Union and was appointed major general U.S. Volunteers by President Abraham Lincoln; headed the Department of Annapolis before assuming command of the Department of the Shenandoah; prevented from reinforcing General G.B. McClellan on the Peninsula by the aggressive actions of General T.J. Jackson's Confederates in

the Shenandoah Valley; defeated Jackson at Kernstown, Virginia, in March 1862, but fared poorly in subsequent actions; assigned to command the Second Corps in General John Pope's newly-formed Army of Virginia; defeated by Jackson at Cedar Mountain during the Second Bull Run Campaign in August 1862; after Pope's army was dismantled, Banks headed briefly the Military District of Washington before assuming command of the Department of the Gulf; conducted a costly operation against Port Hudson, which fell only after Vicksburg's capture left it untenable; directed the marginally successful Bayou Teche Expedition in the fall of 1863; following the failure of his Red River Expedition in 1864, Banks was relieved by General E.R.S. Canby; received thanks of Congress for Port Hudson; mustered out of volunteer service in 1865; returned to Congress where he served six more terms (not consecutively); declining health forced his retirement from Congress in 1890; he died in Massachusetts in 1894. General Banks was among the most active of the higher-ranking "political" generals. He was consistently placed in command positions that were beyond his abilities; his personal courage, devotion, and tenacity could not overcome his lack of military training.

The hopes of Hamilton, Atkinson, and their allies now rested on a smaller Federal expedition to capture Galveston. A naval force of five ships steamed into Galveston harbor in early October and demanded the island city's surrender. The outgunned Confederates meekly complied after withdrawing their artillery, men, and equipment to the nearby mainland. Thus, a handful of Union warships and three companies of a Massachusetts infantry regiment represented the only Federal presence in Texas in late 1862. Even that small toehold was eliminated before dawn on New Year's Day, 1863, when Confederate Brigadier General John B. Magruder surprised the Federals on Galveston Island with a combined infantry and naval assault, captured two Union ships and most of the occupation force, and reclaimed Galveston for the Confederacy.

A.J. Hamilton and his Texas government in exile were left to cool their heels in New Orleans while the Federal government tried to find a way to capture Vicksburg, Port Hudson, and the Mississippi River valley. Until then, Texas would have to wait again. Still, plans and proposals for taking Texas flew back and forth between New Orleans and Washington during the winter, spring, and summer of 1863. Major General Henry W. Halleck, McClellan's successor as general in chief of all Federal armies, exchanged several messages with General Banks in New Orleans, proposing an invasion of Texas as soon as the Mississippi River could be secured for the Union. Halleck's idea was to reach Texas by way of the Red River, a tributary of the Mississippi that cuts diagonally across Louisiana from its northwest corner to the central part of the state. The Red River, Halleck believed, would provide a secure logistical line for an invading Federal army and lead straight to the headquarters of the Confederate Trans-Mississippi Department at Shreveport in northwest Louisiana.

To the great relief of the Texas Unionists and the cotton lobby, two events in the summer of 1863 moved the Texas project forward very abruptly. In June, as Robert E. Lee's gray columns moved toward Gettysburg and while Ulysses S. Grant's blue masses pressed closer to Vicksburg, a French army of 35,000 men sliced through Mexico, occupied the capital city, deposed Mexican President Benito Juárez, and established a French-made government in the halls of Montezuma. This direct slap at the Monroe Doctrine—a United States warning to Europe to keep hands off the Western Hemisphere—and the potential for French-Confederate collusion against the United States got the close attention of the White House.

Then, a few weeks afterward, in early July, Grant's long struggle to grasp control of the Mississippi River finally ended with the capture of Vicksburg. Less than a week later, the last Confederate stronghold on the Mississippi, Port Hudson near Baton Rouge, surrendered, opening the river from its source to its mouth for Northern commerce and splitting the Confederacy in two. Thus, with his higher priority of the Mississippi River now in his pocket, with the Texas lobby still buzzing around Washington, and with a potential new threat looming south of the Rio Grande, President Lincoln determined to let loose the Union Army on the Lone Star State.

The telegraph lines between New Orleans and Washington began crackling with plans and ideas for the invasion of Texas, but now everything was more urgent. General Halleck pushed the idea of an invasion up the Red River toward Shreveport and then into northeastern Texas. Sending a Federal army up the Red River would not only break up the headquarters of the Trans-Mississippi Department; it would also doubtless gather in thousands of bales of Louisiana and Texas cotton for New England textile mills and plant the U.S. flag in Texas as a warning to the French in Mexico.

General Banks, who had earned his general's commission on the strength of his political muscle, was unencumbered by any military training and had, so far in the war, demonstrated no apparent military talent. Confederate General Thomas J.

"Stonewall" Jackson had chased him up and down the Shenandoah Valley of Virginia a year earlier, and Southern soldiers had nicknamed him "Jackson's commissary" for his propensity to lose mountains of supplies to the Virginian. Still, he was a powerful political figure in New England, and President Lincoln was determined to get something out of him sooner or later. So Banks would organize the Texas expedition.

To Halleck's consternation, Banks preferred a different route for the invasion. The Red River, he complained, was too low that summer to admit deep-draft Union gunboats and supply ships. That would leave his army stranded in the piney

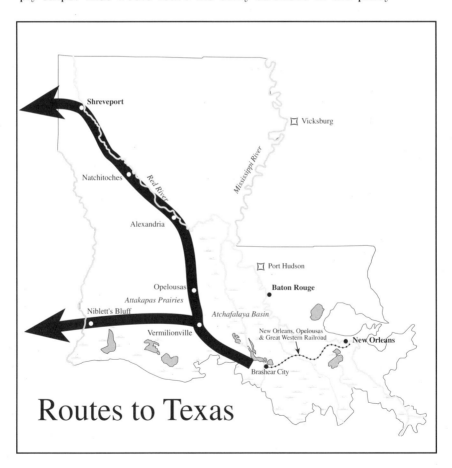

Routes to Texas

woods of northwestern Louisiana without logistical and fire support. Better, he thought, to go directly at the Texas coastline. The brief Federal occupation of Galveston the previous fall had probably led the Confederates to strengthen that point, Banks reasoned. His best chance, he thought, was to put a strong landing force ashore somewhere away from Galveston, but not too far, and then move quickly overland to capture Houston and Galveston, the transportation and trade centers of the state. With those cities in hand, he would control the most important military targets in the state and be in a position to warn off the French in nearby Mexico.

In September, then, General Banks sent a seaborne force of 5,000 men under Major General William B. Franklin from New Orleans to Sabine Pass at the southeast corner of Texas on the Louisiana border. The plan was to land near the lightly defended mouth of the Sabine River and strike quickly overland to capture Galveston and Houston. Franklin, an accomplished cadet at West Point (first in Ulysses Grant's Class of 1843) and an excellent engineer, was less successful as a field commander. His hesitation at the Battle of Fredericksburg in Virginia the previous December had contributed significantly to the Union defeat there, and his record in the Department of the Gulf would earn him no laurels. Through a series of blunders, some by the naval commanders at the scene and some by Franklin, the entire Federal fleet was sent scurrying back to New Orleans after forty-seven Confederate artillerists, commanded by a twenty-five-year-old lieutenant, disabled and captured two gunboats and inflicted 380 casualties on the Union invading force.

By the fall of 1863, then, twenty years of dreaming and scheming about Texas had come to nothing. The Confederates still controlled the state, the slaves were still in bondage, New England mills still needed Texas cotton, the French were still looming next door in Mexico, and Andrew Hamilton's Unionist government was still waiting, waiting in New Orleans. Federal

William B. Franklin: born Pennsylvania 1823; graduated U.S. Military Academy 1843, first in his class of forty-three that included U.S. Grant; brevetted 2d lieutenant assigned to engineers; part of Great Lakes survey team 1843–45; with Philip Kearney's Rocky Mountain expedition 1846; won two brevets for Mexican War service, including one for gallantry at Buena Vista; from 1848 to 1861 he was involved in numerous engineering projects, among these was the construction of a new dome for the national capitol; taught engineering at West Point; gained slow but steady promotion reaching captain in 1857; at the outbreak of the Civil War he was commissioned colonel of the 12th U.S. Infantry and brigadier general U.S. Volunteers shortly thereafter; commanded a brigade at First Bull Run and a division in the Washington defenses following that debacle; commanded a division and then the Sixth Corps during the Peninsular Campaign; promoted to major general U.S. Volunteers July 1862; directed the Sixth Corps during the Maryland Campaign and was conspicuously involved at Crampton's Gap, South Mountain, and Antietam, September 1862; commanded the Left Grand Division at Fredericksburg, after which he was accused by General Ambrose Burnside of failing to follow orders; although not disciplined, his career was irreparably damaged; sent West, he commanded the Nineteenth Corps in General N.P. Banks's Red River Expedition during which he was twice wounded, ending his field service; brevetted brigadier general U.S. Army for his actions in the Peninsular Campaign and major general U.S. Army for war service, he was retired in 1866; from then until 1888, he was an executive with Colt's Firearms Manufacturing Company; he also supervised the construction of the Connecticut state capitol and held a variety of public offices until his death at Hartford in 1903. Although he owned a relatively solid service record, General Franklin could not overcome the stigma of the disaster at Fredericksburg.

officials in Washington were not about to give up on Texas, however, and they would try again on a larger scale than ever before.

2
INTO THE BAYOU COUNTRY

If not a highly skilled military man, General Banks was at least a highly optimistic one, and he immediately began planning another invasion of Texas after the failure of the Sabine Pass expedition. At his headquarters in New Orleans, he and his staff hauled out their maps of Louisiana, pondered the Red River route once again, and then began scanning the features of southern Louisiana between the Mississippi River and the Texas border, the Teche and prairie country of the Cajuns.

General Banks and his officers were quite familiar with the country along the banks of Bayou Teche, which flows southward from central Louisiana. The general had marched his army from New Orleans up the Teche the previous spring to cut the Confederacy's trans-Mississippi supply line to Port Hudson. After clearing the Teche country of Confederate troops and occupying Alexandria on the Red River, Banks had turned eastward to besiege Port Hudson while Grant closed in on Vicksburg. Now that Vicksburg and Port Hudson had fallen and the Mississippi was firmly under Union control, Banks considered how he might use the Teche again, this time to get at Texas.

Bayou Teche was on the eastern edge of a great expanse of prairies that stretched to the Texas border. Along that bayou and in the tributaries and marshes of the great Atchafalaya River basin east of the Teche lived most of Louisiana's French-Catholic Cajun population (descendants of French exiles from British Canada during the eighteenth century). The Teche valley was one of the richest regions of plantation Louisiana. Its large sugar plantations and prosperous farms provided valuable manpower and supplies for the Confederate war effort. On the sparsely settled prairies west of the Teche, Cajun farmers raised a few cattle and generally followed a subsistence lifestyle. Their small farms had been virtually untouched by the war, and an invading army might find provisions in their fields and barns. Unfortunately for any invader, their settlements and farms were so far apart that, no matter how untouched they were, they would provide little food or fiber for cold and hungry soldiers.

General Banks, having doubts about the Red River route to northeastern Texas, and his subordinates, having botched the Sabine Pass landing, determined in September 1863 to cross the Mississippi at New Orleans, move westward overland by rail to Brashear City (now Morgan City), then march up Bayou Teche as they had the previous spring. Somewhere on his way up the Teche, Banks would decide either to continue northward to Alexandria and the Red River country (thereby satisfying his superior, General Halleck) or to turn westward across the prairies toward Niblett's Bluff on the Texas border. Once there, he could dash upon Houston and Galveston, wave the American flag under French noses, gather cotton bales by the thousands, and advance the Union cause of freedom.

The only Confederates in his way would be the ragged

legions of Major General Richard Taylor, son of former United States President Zachary Taylor and former brother-in-law of Confederate President Jefferson Davis. A well-educated and wealthy sugar planter, Taylor was, like Banks, a civilian turned soldier. Unlike Banks, however, Taylor had a natural talent for

Richard Taylor: born Kentucky 1826; son of President and Mexican War hero Zachary Taylor and brother-in-law of Confederate President Jefferson Davis; studied at Yale; became a successful sugar planter in Louisiana; elected colonel 9th Louisiana Infantry at the outbreak of the Civil War and went with the regiment to Virginia, arriving too late for First Manassas; promoted to brigadier general 1861; commanded the Louisiana Brigade in Major General Thomas J. "Stonewall" Jackson's Shenandoah Valley Campaign of 1862; present but not active during the Seven Days' Battles before Richmond; promoted to major general and assigned to command the District of Western Louisiana in 1862; unsuccessfully opposed Major General Nathaniel P. Banks' Bayou Teche Expedition in 1863, but turned back Banks' Red River Expedition the following spring; after a heated exchange in which he criticized his commander, General E. Kirby Smith, for not following up this success, he asked to be relieved; he was, however, promoted to lieutenant general and assigned to command the Department of Alabama, Mississippi, and East Louisiana; following the disaster at Nashville, he temporarily succeeded General John B. Hood in command of the Army of Tennessee, most of which he forwarded to the  Carolinas to oppose Major General William T. Sherman's advance; after the fall of Mobile he surrendered the last remaining Confederate force east of the Mississippi to Major General E.R.S. Canby on May 4, 1865; following the war he was active in Democratic politics and vigorously opposed Reconstruction policies; died at New York in 1879. That year he published *Destruction and Reconstruction*, one of the finest participant memoirs to be produced. Without any formal military training, General Taylor proved to be a most able commander. The Confederate repulse of the Red River Expedition, though largely overlooked, was a major achievement.

military matters. He had been a brigade commander under Stonewall Jackson during the famous Valley Campaign of 1862 and had become accustomed to seeing the back of Nathaniel P. Banks. Well versed in the classics and modern literature, always dressed in the finest suits, imperious to subordinates who failed to show proper respect, and confident in his abilities, Taylor displayed little respect for his Massachusetts-born opponent. The dapper Confederate general was still fuming over his unavoidable springtime retreat before Banks's superi-

John G. Walker: born Missouri 1822; received his early education at the Jesuit College in St. Louis; commissioned directly into the U.S. Army in 1846, he served during the war with Mexico and had attained the rank of captain by the time he resigned in 1861 to enter Confederate service; commissioned major of cavalry in the regular Confederate Army, and was made brigadier general early in 1862; dis-

tinguished himself with the Army of Northern Virginia through the Maryland Campaign, and was promoted major general in November 1862; his division of two brigades took possession of Loudon Heights in the operations against Harper's Ferry in September 1862, and subsequently rendered gallant service during the Battle of Sharpsburg; at this juncture he was transferred to the Trans-Mississippi Department, where he assumed command of the Texas Infantry Division; after participating in the Red River Campaign, he relieved General Richard Taylor in the District of West Louisiana; at the close of the war he was in command of a division in the District of Texas, New Mexico, and Arizona, his troops being composed at the time of Steele's, Bee's, and Bagby's cavalry divisions, Cooper's Indians, and Slaughter's Brigade. Walker went to Mexico without waiting for his personal parole at the end of hostilities; later he served as U.S. consul general at Bogota, Columbia, and as special commissioner to the South American republics on behalf of the Pan-American Convention; he died at Washington, D.C., in 1893, and is buried in Winchester, Virginia.

or forces along the Teche, and he looked forward to another meeting with the commander of the Federal Department of the Gulf.

Unfortunately for Taylor, his resources would not allow him to fight a stand-up, pitched battle against any sizable Union army. The bulk of his small army of 8,400 men was composed of mostly untested Texas infantry, commanded by Major General John G. Walker. A native of Missouri and a career officer in the United States Army before the war, Walker had commanded a small division at the bloody Battle of Antietam in western Maryland a year earlier. His hard fighting and fast marching in the eastern theater had earned him a major-generalship and the command of what became known as Walker's Texas Division in 1863. Only one of his three brigades had seen any action at all in this war, and that for only a few hours, at the assault on Milliken's Bend above Vicksburg the previous June. Altogether, his division numbered about 4,000 men in the fall of 1863.

A smaller division of Louisiana troops under Brigadier General Jean Jacques Alfred Alexander Mouton included roughly 2,400 men present for duty. A graduate of West Point (Class of 1850), son of former Louisiana governor and U.S. senator Alfred Mouton, and wounded veteran of the bloody affair at Shiloh, Mouton boasted a pedigree almost as distinguished as Taylor's.

The cavalry of this little army numbered about 2,000 Texans under the command of another colorful figure in Confederate history, Brigadier General Thomas Green. Virginia-born and Tennessee-educated, Green was better known for his military skills than for his accomplishments in his chosen profession, the law. A veteran of the Battle of San Jacinto in the Texas Revolution and a famed Indian fighter on the Texas frontier before the war, Green had also fought in Mexico under General Zachary Taylor, had participated in the Confederate invasion of New Mexico early in the Civil War, and had helped to liberate Galveston from Yankee control on New Year's Day. A cavalry leader with that much military experience and aggressive instinct might prove to be a formidable adversary.

General Banks had forced Taylor, Mouton, and Green back along the Teche on his way to Alexandria the previous spring,

Cadwallader C. Washburn: born Maine 1818; as a young man Washburn moved to Mineral Point, Wisconsin, where he opened a law office in 1842; he also engaged in banking, land speculation, lumbering, and other highly profitable enterprises; in 1854 he was elected as a Republican to the U.S. House of Representatives, joining for a time his brothers Elihu and Israel; Washburn left Congress after three terms, but participated in the 1861 Washington Peace Conference, following the outbreak of the Civil War he was commissioned into the volunteer army in February 1862 as colonel of the 2d Wisconsin Cavalry; after early service in Missouri, Washburn was elevated to brigadier general of volunteers in July 1862 and major general in March 1863 (to rank from November 1862); he commanded a cavalry division in the Trans-Mississippi and in the Army of the Tennessee; in early 1863 he conducted the Yazoo Pass Expedition in a preliminary move against Vicksburg; in the final stage of that campaign he commanded a three-division detachment; after the fall of Vicksburg he periodically directed the Thirteenth Corps in the Department of the Gulf and, in April 1864, became commander of the District of West Tennessee, a position he held for the balance of the war; Washburn resigned in May 1865; after the war he returned to Congress for two terms and later founded the company that became General Mills; this, combined with his other endeavors, helped Washburn build a considerable fortune; he died at Eureka Springs, Arkansas, in 1882.

Although he proved himself a competent soldier, Washburn's Civil War career doubtless benefitted from his brother's strong connections—Elihu Washburne (he added the e to the family name) was both a close confidant of President Abraham Lincoln and a strong supporter of General U.S. Grant.

however, and the Union general was convinced he could do it again in the fall. For the great Texas Overland Expedition, he put together a formidable army of more than 30,000 men, the largest Federal army assembled in the Trans-Mississippi during the entire war. The largest unit of Banks's expedition was the Thirteenth Army Corps, commanded by Major General Cadwallader C. Washburn, a Maine native who had moved to Wisconsin in the 1840s and become a prosperous lawyer and businessman. Washburn's two brothers, Israel and Elihu, were very prominent in Northern politics. Israel was the wartime Governor of Maine, and Elihu was a tough Radical Republican ally of Thaddeus Stevens. Indeed, it was Elihu who had selected Ulysses S. Grant for a brigadier-generalship in 1861. General Washburn himself would later serve in the U.S. House of Representatives and hold the governorship of Wisconsin.

The men of his corps, tough Western veterans of the Vicksburg campaign, had recently been transferred to the Department of the Gulf. Accustomed to success and little bothered by the finer points of gentlemanly combat, the men of the Thirteenth Corps believed nothing and nobody could stand in their way, certainly not the ragged Trans-Mississippi Confederates. While the Thirteenth Corps carried 20,500 soldiers on its rolls in the fall of 1863, its actual strength in men present for duty was somewhat less. Even at that, Washburn's corps alone was more than double the size of Taylor's whole army.

Traveling with the Westerners of the Thirteenth Corps in the overland invasion would be the Nineteenth Army Corps, composed mainly of Easterners from Massachusetts, New York, and Pennsylvania. Led by Major General William B. Franklin, the kindly but star-crossed commander of the Sabine Pass expedition, this corps, too, had reason to be proud of its history. While their counterparts had taken Vicksburg, the men of the Nineteenth Corps could boast of taking Port Hudson. Indeed, the corps had suffered more than 4,300 casualties in the Port Hudson Campaign. Nearly 10,000 strong in the fall of 1863, they were the men who had pushed Taylor's Confederates up the Teche several months earlier and were therefore familiar with the territory.

The cavalry division assigned to the overland expedition was commanded by Brigadier General Albert L. Lee, a New Yorker by birth who had migrated to Kansas before the war and risen quickly in the legal profession to serve on the new

Albert L. Lee: born New York 1834; graduated from Union College in Schenectady, New York, in 1853, Lee studied law and eventually moved to Kansas; in 1861 he became an associate justice of the Kansas Supreme Court, but resigned to enter the volunteer army following the outbreak of the Civil War; commissioned a major in the 7th Kansas Cavalry, Lee saw limited action in Kansas and Missouri before commanding a brigade at Corinth, Mississippi, in October 1862; he led a cavalry

brigade in the Army of the Tennessee in the early stages of the Vicksburg Campaign and was promoted to brigadier general, U.S. Volunteers, in April 1863 (to rank from November 1862); during the move on Vicksburg, Lee served as acting chief of staff to General John A. McClernand and, following the wounding of General Peter Osterhaus, commanded the Ninth Division, Thirteenth Corps, Army of the Tennessee, at Big Black River on 17 May 1863; two days later, leading an infantry brigade in an assault on Vicksburg, Lee was wounded in the fact and head; returning to duty in July, he filled various division commands until selected to head the Cavalry Division of the Department of the Gulf in September; Lee fared poorly commanding the cavalry in General N.P. Banks's disastrous Red River Expedition in the spring of 1864; although Lee retained his command for a time, his troubled relationship with Banks's successor, General E.R.S. Canby, eventually cost him his job; ostracized by Canby, Lee resigned in May 1865. After the war, he travelled extensively in Europe and engaged in business in New York City. General Lee died in New York in 1907.

state's Supreme Court. His troopers were mainly Midwesterners, but a few regiments hailed from other states. One of those other regiments, the 1st Texas Cavalry (U.S.), included many Texas Unionists hoping to lead the invasion into their home state. Their colonel, Edmund J. Davis, would be elected to the Texas governorship during radical Reconstruction after

Edmund J. Davis: born Florida 1827; moved with his widowed mother to Texas in 1838 settling first in Galveston; studied law in Corpus Christi and later practiced in Laredo, Corpus Christi, and Brownsville; served as deputy collector of customs with headquarters at Laredo from 1850 to 1852; elected district attorney at Brownsville in 1853, and made judge of the district from 1854 to 1861, which included all of the Texas portion of the lower Rio Grande Valley; he held that position until he was defeated for election to the Secession Convention at the outbreak of the Civil War; his friends attributed to that defeat his alienation from the Confederate cause; he organized a regiment of cavalry composed mainly of Unionists who had escaped from Texas into Mexico and, while recruiting for his regiment near Matamoros, was captured by a band of Confederates and narrowly escaped hanging; his regiment spent most of the war period in Louisiana, but Davis led the unsuccessful Union attack on Laredo in 1864; he was made a brigadier general of U.S. volunteers in November 1864; a delegate to the Texas constitutional convention of 1866 and president of the convention of 1869; among other proposals, he adovcated unrestricted black suffrage, the disfranchisement of some ex-Confederates, and the division of Texas into more

than one state; elected governor in 1869 with Federal military support, Davis exercised great power for the duration of his term, for example, having authority to appoint over eight thousand state and local employees; ousted by a majority of forty thousand Democratic votes in 1873, he appealed unsuccessfully to President U.S. Grant to be sustained in office; Davis then resumed his law practice in Austin, Texas, where he died in 1883; he is buried in the State Cemetery.

the war. Altogether, Lee's cavalry columns included nearly 4,000 men.

General Banks, eager to strike at Texas and win the military glory that had always eluded him, began ferrying these corps and brigades across the Mississippi at New Orleans early on Sunday morning, September 13. The crowded ferries, including small vessels pressed into service and large river steamers, continued their to-and-fro movements into early October as additional regiments were prepared and brought up to the river bank. If the Army of the Gulf had been lined up on a single road, with its tens of thousands of men and hundreds of supply and munition wagons in tow, it would have stretched nearly forty miles long. As it was, some regiments crossed the river and took the trains westward while others were still marching down Canal Street in New Orleans and still others were yet in their camps, packing and preparing for another push toward Texas. General Banks had put a formidable military machine in motion.

Once across the river at Algiers, the men of the various regiments boarded flatcars on the New Orleans, Opelousas and Great Western Railroad for the eighty-mile trip to Brashear City on the Atchafalaya River. Stacked as high and as deep as the cars would allow, the men scrambled for places on, in, and under wagons and artillery pieces, atop boxes and barrels and bags, and anywhere space could be found. There was the usual amount of grousing about the stupidity of the government, but these were veterans, and they had seen far worse in the trenches around Vicksburg and Port Hudson. Compared to that, this was a lark.

The locomotives huffed and wheezed and pulled away from the station at Algiers and then stayed close to the river for several miles before veering away to the west. Stopping every few miles to load or unload passengers and cargo, the train eventually entered a dark and humid swamp. One soldier described the strange sights: "The long stretches of cypress swamps, thickets of Spanish bayonets, poisoned black waters overlaid with plants, rank and rampant vegetation, luxuriant foliage knit upon vines leaping from tree to tree, funereal with the ever present Spanish moss, furnished wonderfully new scenery to our Northern eyes."

After too many stops to remember, the crowded rail cars finally pulled into the station at Brashear City on the east bank of the Atchafalaya. The little village could hardly be called a city. An unimpressive collection of cattle pens, train facilities, and small stores and shops, the settlement had suffered the fate of so many other towns caught in the path of war. Burned-out buildings, rubble, and ugly earthworks littered the landscape. The population of Brashear City soon doubled, tripled, quadrupled, and soared beyond imagination as more trains arrived with more Yankee regiments and brigades, more boxes and barrels, more artillery pieces and wagons, more horses and mules. The men spread out over the surrounding countryside, raising tents, digging latrines, setting up supply dumps, starting camp fires, and generally overwhelming the whole area. And then more of them chugged in from the east on the tracks of the New Orleans, Opelousas and Great Western. There seemed to be no end of them. For three weeks the trains pulled in, unloaded, and returned to Algiers for yet another load of Yankees.

Lurking Confederate scouts, peering through their spyglasses, must have wondered how their small army could stop such a collection of men and war material. The Trans-Mississippi had never seen such a sight. Texas Unionists on the expedition and the Texas lobby in Washington must have breathed a sigh of relief. Now that Banks had moved into the bayou country on his way west, the Lone Star State finally seemed within their reach.

3
ON TO TEXAS

General Banks's heavy blue columns crossed the Atchafalaya at Brashear City in late September and established more camps across the river, in and around Berwick City, another dilapidated village flattering itself with a grandiose name, and farther north, along the west bank of Bayou Teche. Under orders from General Banks, still in New Orleans, the Federal brigades and divisions finally broke camp early on October 3 and began inching up the Teche, which flows into the Atchafalaya just north of Berwick. The morning was cool, crisp, and clear, a welcome change from the rain and humidity that had hung over their camps for several days, and the men were in correspondingly high spirits. It was up the Teche and on to Texas for the confident veterans of the Thirteenth and Nineteenth army corps.

The men of these two corps would clash with each other almost as much as with the elusive Confederates, who seemed

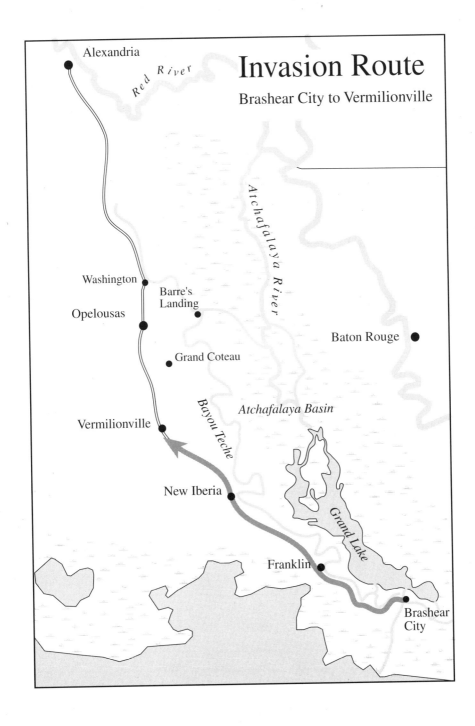

Alexandria

Red River

Invasion Route
Brashear City to Vermilionville

Atchafalaya River

Washington

Barre's
Landing

Opelousas

Baton Rouge

Grand Coteau

Atchafalaya Basin

Bayou Teche

Vermilionville

New Iberia

Grand Lake

Franklin

Brashear
City

to vanish before them as they marched. Each corps had a string of victories to its credit, and naturally, each felt its contribution was more important to the overall war effort. In addition, the regiments from the two corps originated in different parts of the country. The Easterners of the Nineteenth Corps sniffed at the rough, raw Westerners of the Thirteenth, and the latter poked fun at the starched collars and formality of the Easterners.

A surgeon in a New York regiment acknowledged the fighting qualities of the Westerners but noted that "they had a wonderful disregard of personal appearance, wearing all manner of dirty and outlandish costumes. They also took a special delight in destroying every species of rebel property that came within their reach, whether serviceable to them or not." The Easterners could hardly tolerate the boastful Westerners. "They were... arrant braggarts," the New Yorker fumed, "continually dilating upon their wonderful achievements, and forever depreciating the laudable efforts of others." The men from Indiana and Illinois and Wisconsin had an equally low opinion of the Easterners. The Westerners boasted that they had come to the Trans-Mississippi to show the New Yorkers and New Englanders how to fight, that they would wipe out resistance west of the Mississippi if only the fancy uniforms of the East would stay out of the way. Catcalls, aspersions, and curses flew back and forth between the two groups, and when their officers were not present, men from the two sections traded knuckles and bloody noses as well. "I think either side would rather shoot at each other than at the Johnnies," one soldier observed.

The bitterness between the two corps only increased the longer they marched together. It became so destructive of morale that the generals in both units finally decided to separate them, on the march and in camp. As the army wound its way up the west bank of the Teche, the men of the Nineteenth Corps were kept well ahead of their tormentors in the

Thirteenth. General Franklin, who would eventually head the whole Overland Expedition, even considered mixing the regiments and brigades of the two corps into a single corps to eliminate this internal friction. Perhaps if the regional corps distinctions were eliminated, harmony would prevail. The two units, he sighed, "are from different sections of the country, do not know each other, and are consequently jealous of each other." Franklin never followed through on his idea, and sectional tensions continued to plague his army throughout the campaign.

The soldiers of the Nineteenth Corps had taken this same route up the Teche the preceding spring, chasing Taylor, Mouton, and Green all the way to Alexandria in the central part of the state. These Federals were therefore familiar with the sights and sounds of the Teche country. The Westerners coming along behind them, however, had been sloshing through the swamps west of Vicksburg and fighting their way into central Mississippi that spring, and they were seeing the bayou country of south Louisiana for the first time. They found the scenes along the Teche exotic almost beyond description. The huge sugarcane fields, the burned-out plantations, plants and animals foreign to the North, the French language of the Cajuns—all caught the attention of the men in blue as they trudged up the road bordering the bayou. And since Taylor's outnumbered Confederate infantry stayed well away from them and Green's darting cavalry made only occasional, brief appearances, the soldiers of the Federal army had plenty of time to enjoy the sights.

An Indiana man described one of his regiment's first stops on the march up the Teche: "On the edge of the bayou, we camped for the night, where, as the night closed in, great long-legged, blood-thirsty gallinippers [mosquitoes] made their appearance, and we had to skirmish and fight to save our very heart's blood; and as the dark, still hours passed by, we could hear in the swamps near us the bellowing of alligators, like a herd of lost bulls."

Some of the wondrous sensory experiences of south

Louisiana were more pleasant. An Iowa soldier marveled at the "orange groves and sugar plantations innumerable, and warehouses filled with sugar.:" Mile after mile, the Westerners spied the brick smokestacks of plantation sugar houses along the bayou. A correspondent for the *New York Herald*, traveling along with the soldiers, also noted the beauty of the country-side: "Nowhere in the South, before the war, was there such a country for natural beauty and richness of soil, as this 'paradise of the South,' while the palatial residences of the planters rising...out of the shrubbery which surrounded them, gave the whole scenery an air of unparalleled grandeur. ..."

Those who took a second glance, however, noted that many of the fine estates had been burned or sacked earlier in the war. The *Herald's* reporter described a common scene along the route of march: "Those mansions are now silent and deserted, the plantations are desolate and overgrown with weeds and briers, while the cottages of the negroes are tenantless and fast falling to ruin. I noticed but two or three of these plantations under cultivation...."

One planter, Judge William Taylor Palfrey, described the fate of his property when the Nineteenth Corps had passed through the preceding spring. Not only had Federal soldiers invaded his home and pitched their tents on his lawn; they had destroyed property whether they needed it or not. "They used the lumber of my remaining buildings for fuel and... small shelters. The Federal troops burned, through mischievious wantoness, several of the venerable live-oak trees which adorned my front lawn, measuring 9 feet in diameter." Now the old planter (ironically, a Massachusetts native) played host to the even rougher soldiers of the Thirteenth Corps in October. Some of the men barged into the big house and into the dining room, where they found the judge's wife eating her dinner. They walked around the table, grabbing food from the plates and doubtless scaring the mistress badly, before moving on to other adventures.

The Westerners were not the only unwelcome guests along the Teche, however. On the same day that the judge's dining room was invaded, another local resident a few miles up the road in Centerville suffered at the hands of the Nineteenth Corps. Some New York soldiers, accompanied by their colonel, broke down the doors of a dry-goods warehouse, ostensibly to search for lurking rebels. Finding none, they proceeded to sack the store, throwing what merchandise they did not take with them into the Teche. Reuben Scott of the 67th Indiana Infantry, recalling recent fires that had broken out in the wake of his unit, admitted with a wink that "It seemed that our presence sometimes created *spontaneous combustion.*" Although the Federal generals had explicitly prohibited looting and abuse of non-hostile civilians, such scenes were repeated frequently along the army's path. Louisiana's civilians learned to flee or suffer the consequences.

Even the wildlife along the Teche felt the hand of war. At each hourly rest stop on their march, some soldiers took the opportunity to jog over to the bayou and take potshots at sleepy alligators sunning themselves on the muddy banks. A Wisconsin war correspondent noted that the soldiers "cannot resist the temptation of a philosophical experiment—the visible effect of impinging lead upon a tough, horny hide." The men of the Thirteenth Corps had less of this fun than their counterparts farther up the road, however. "We saw legions of dead alligators," one Westerner wrote, "but found few live ones for us to try our Enfield rifles upon." The sharpshooters of the East had already passed this way.

While the Federal army marched up the roads bordering the Teche to the tune of "The Star-Spangled Banner" and "Rally 'Round the Flag," General Taylor and his Confederate brigades stayed well away to the north, between Alexandria and Opelousas. If Taylor's Confederate foot soldiers had been able to watch the Federal sport of alligator shooting, they would doubtless have been envious. The Southerners had orders to

Engagement with a Rebel Alligator

conserve ammunition, to fire their weapons only upon a direct command, and to account each Thursday for every cartridge issued to them the previous week or pay the Confederate States of America forty cents per cartridge. The wildlife near Taylor's army was safe.

While General Taylor's men counted their cartridges, their officers tried to decipher the enemy's intentions. On October 6 Taylor reported to Trans-Mississippi headquarters that "the enemy is advancing in very large force. Whether it is his intention to march to the Red River Valley before going to Texas has not yet been developed...." In another dispatch sent the same day, Taylor reminded his superiors that the Federals "can strike out [to the west] by the road from Vermilionville, or from New Iberia, via Abbeville, to Niblett's Bluff [on the Texas border]." To be safe, Taylor began to remove his army's stores from Alexandria.

Edmund Kirby Smith: born Florida 1824; graduated from the U.S. Military Academy in 1845, twenty-fifth in his class of forty-one; commissioned 2d lieutenant of infantry; earned brevets to 1st lieutenant and captain in the Mexican War;

taught mathematics at West Point from 1849 to 1852; promoted to 1st lieutenant and captain before joining the newly formed 2d Cavalry in 1855; as a major in this elite regiment, he resigned his commission in 1861 to enter Confederate service; commissioned colonel, he served on General J.E. Johnston's staff in the Shenandoah Valley; brigadier general June 1861; led troops and was wounded at First Manassas; elevated to major general in October 1861; assigned to command the Department of East Tennessee in March 1862; in conjunction with General Braxton Bragg, invaded Kentucky in the summer of 1862; after his victory at Richmond, the campaign ended after Bragg's inconclusive actions at Perryville; promoted to lieutenant general in October 1862, Smith was ordered

Two days later, Taylor's superior, Lieutenant General Edmund Kirby Smith, commander of the entire Confederate Trans-Mississippi Department, expressed doubts that Banks would try the Red River route: "The fall and winter rains soon set in, and the difficulties of campaigning in this upper country become almost insurmountable." If, on the other hand, the Federals turned west across the prairies, Smith ordered Taylor to strike at their flanks while other Confederate forces in Texas marshaled at the Louisiana border to stop them at Niblett's Bluff.

The soldiers in Taylor's ranks were prepared for a fight in either direction. Captain Elijah Petty of the 17th Texas Infantry in Walker's Division wrote to his wife that "we are ready, eager and anxious for a fight and aint at all particular when or how it comes. Our army is in good health, fine spirits and good moral[e]...and if the fight does come off the federal

to the Trans-Mississippi Department; he assumed command there in February; the fall of Vicksburg in July 1863 left the Trans-Mississippi cut off from the rest of the Confederacy; the isolated department became known as "Kirby Smithdom" in which the general exercised virtually independent command for the balance of the war; promoted full general in February 1864; in the spring of that year the Federals launched the ambitious Red River Campaign to capture Shreveport, Louisiana; General Richard Taylor directed the repulse of Federal General N.P. Banks's approach at Mansfield and Pleasant Hill while Smith repulsed General Frederick Steele's advance in Arkansas; Taylor, angered by Smith's handling of the campaign, asked to be relieved and was later reassigned; owing to his isolation from the Confederate capital, Smith promoted several generals on his own authority, only a few of which were ever approved and confirmed by President Jefferson Davis and the Confederate Senate; with the collapse of the Confederacy, Smith surrendered the last organized Confederate force to General E.R.S. Canby at Galveston, Texas, in June 1865; fearing arrest, Smith fled to Mexico, returning to the United States several months later; after failing in business, he became president of the University of Nashville; in 1875 he joined the faculty of the University of the South at Sewanee, Tennessee. The last survivor of the eight Confederate generals of full rank, Smith died at Sewanee in 1893.

fur will fly." A fellow Texan in another of Walker's regiments wrote his sister that the Yankees "do not wish to have a general engagement with us unless they can get all the advantage. They think we are too strong for them." Still, most of Taylor's infantrymen had never been in a fight, and thoughts of their mortality inevitably crept into their minds as they awaited developments. Two days after his blustery first letter, Petty tried to prepare his wife for bad news. "If I get killed or taken prisoner be of good cheer. The fates have so decreed it and it is all right. Take care of yourself & my children and raise them as they should be and as I know you are capable. ...Tom Irvine is sick again & has been sent to the rear. This is according to his Mothers wish which was that he should get sick before every fight."

By October 9 Banks's army had driven seventy miles, from Brashear City to Vermilionville (present-day Lafayette), a parish seat and sizable town on the Vermilion River. General Banks himself had come up from New Orleans to observe the crossing of the river and occupation of the town. On the tenth, Federal generals rolled out four batteries, scattered skirmish-

Federals Crossing Vermilion Bayou, October 15, 1863

ers to the front, and put several brigades into line to meet expected resistance at the crossing of the muddy stream. "For about an hour the firing was very warm," the *New York Herald's* correspondent reported, "the booming of the cannon being interspersed with the sharp reports of the muskets...."

While the artillery threw shells into the town across the river, the Unionist Texas cavalry of Colonel Edmund J. Davis, the future Reconstruction governor, splashed across the river on the right of the Federal line, chasing Confederate Texans away from the scene. Tom Green's 500 gray cavalrymen north of the river, dodging artillery shells and awed by the sight of the overwhelming force across the stream, fired only a few shots and wisely left the scene. Federal regiments and batteries then bridged the river and occupied the town. The Texas Overland Expedition was, so far, a great success.

Having conquered Vermilionville, General Banks then left the army to his lieutenants and returned to New Orleans. His fertile mind was now contemplating a two-pronged invasion of Texas. While the Overland Expedition pushed toward the Lone Star State from the east, and thereby drew Confederates in Texas toward the Louisiana border, why not walk in the back door of the state where the opposition would necessarily be feeble—at Brownsville on the Mexican border? Not only would Confederate resistance be negligible at the mouth of the Rio Grande; a Federal occupation of the southernmost point of Texas would be a stern warning to the French in Mexico that the United States would not tolerate any flirtations with the rebels of Richmond and Shreveport.

Federal forces at Brownsville would also effectively shut down the heavy Confederate cotton trade across the border to Matamoros, a trade that supplied much of the Trans-Mississippi's war materiel. And finally, of course, it would allow the long-suffering refugee Unionists of Texas to return home and establish a state government loyal to Washington. From Brownsville, they could then extend their new regime's reaches further inland and, eventually, reassert Federal control over the whole state—especially if the main Union army at Vermilionville could occupy east Texas, whether through Niblett's Bluff or Shreveport.

Banks's scheme, if successful, would certainly realize some of the diplomatic and political objectives of the Texas expedition. The Massachusetts general had apparently not considered all the requirements of his embryonic plan, however. In order for the strategy to succeed, Banks's lieutenants on the Vermilion would have to know they were part of a two-pronged campaign. They would also need some instruction on which route to Texas they should take and when to take it. Close coordination between the generals at Vermilionville and those bound for Brownsville would have to be maintained to keep adequate forces on both vectors. Unfortunately for the Federal officers he left behind at Vermilionville, Banks evidently kept his elaborate scheme to himself. He definitely did not give them specific instructions about how they should proceed next.

So, it was "On to Texas" among the men in the ranks, but their officers were not sure how to get there. This uncertainty and lack of strong direction from above would plague the Federal Army of the Gulf throughout the campaign.

4
THE INVASION STALLS

While General Banks's steamer chugged down the Teche toward Brashear City, his army at Vermilionville crawled slowly northward, covering only ten miles in five days. The delay was partly due to the ever-present Confederate cavalry led by General Tom Green. Hovering on the fringes of the Federal army, always lurking and gathering information—and occasionally striking at isolated foraging parties—the gray horsemen were a constant torment to the northerners. The *New York Herald's* correspondent had complained about the bothersome enemy cavalry even before the blue army had reached Vermilionville. They "assumed an air of defiance, sending their scouts within a short distance of our lines, and making a show of strength which they were not supposed to be possessed of." Edmund J. Davis's Unionist Texas cavalry had sometimes given chase, but the elusive rebels always disappeared, only to reappear later.

If the Federals were frustrated by the gray cavalry, so was General Taylor frustrated by the Union army's careful response to his horsemen. "The enemy moves with the greatest caution," Taylor complained to headquarters. "Nothing can induce

Thomas Green: born Virginia 1814; moved with his family to Tennessee in 1817; attended the University of Nashville and Princeton College in Kentucky; practiced law in Tennessee before relocating to Texas in 1835; in the War for Texas Independence, he fought in the Battle of San Jacinto in 1836; served the Republic of Texas as adjutant general of the army, legislator, and soldier in numerous actions against Indians and Mexicans; captain of Texas volunteers with General Zachary Taylor in the Mexican War; clerk of the Texas Supreme Court from 1841 to 1861; at the outbreak of the Civil War he became colonel of the 5th Texas Cavalry; in General Henry Hopkins Sibley's 1862 invasion of New Mexico he commanded

Confederate forces at Valverde and performed capably throughout the disastrous campaign; in January 1863 he participated in the recapture of Galveston; later that year Sibley's Brigade joined General Richard Taylor's command in Louisiana to oppose General N. P. Banks's Bayou Teche Expedition; when Sibley fell ill, Green assumed direction of the brigade; promoted to brigadier general in May 1863; led the brigade in operations associated with the defense of Vicksburg; in southern Louisiana, he defeated Federal forces at Bayous La Fourche, Fordoche, and Bourbeau after which Taylor recommended Green's promotion to major general; Green's hard-riding troopers were sent back to Texas late in 1863 to oppose a threatened Federal invasion; returned to Louisiana in the spring of 1864 in response to Banks's drive up the Red River; conspicuously engaged at Mansfield and Pleasant Hill; as the Federals retreated, Green, now commanding a cavalry division, was dispatched to harass Union gunboats on the Red; in a assault on the gunboat Osage at Blair's Landing on October 12, Green was killed. General Taylor was lavish in his praise of Green and considered the loss of the Texan "irreparable." General Green indeed owned an impressive record, much of which was won against long odds. His brother-in-law was Confederate General James P. Major.

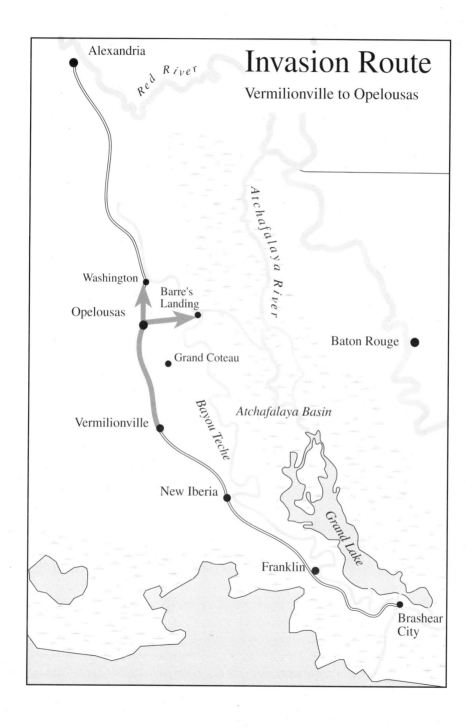

Alexandria

Red River

Invasion Route
Vermilionville to Opelousas

Atchafalaya River

Washington

Barre's
Landing

Opelousas

Grand Coteau

Baton Rouge

Atchafalaya Basin

Bayou Teche

Vermilionville

New Iberia

Grand Lake

Franklin

Brashear
City

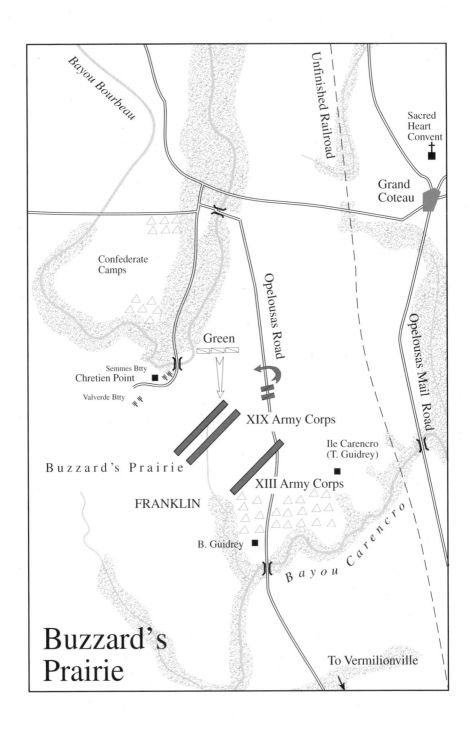

his cavalry to separate 500 yards from his infantry supports."

Finally, shortly after dawn on October 15, Green's cavalry made a stand of sorts on a large prairie about ten miles north of Vermilionville. On the wooded northern edge of the opening, called Buzzard's Prairie, was a muddy stream called Bayou Bourbeau, and backing up to the bayou was a large plantation house, Chretien Point. From the second-floor gallery of the columned mansion, Green's scouts watched the Federal Nineteenth Corps draw up from the south and slowly enter the open plain. On the grounds in front of the house, along its fence facing the prairie, and in slave cabins near the mansion, three regiments of Texas cavalrymen loaded their carbines and pistols. At their far left was the 1st Regular Confederate Battery, commanded by Captain Oliver Semmes (son of the famous sea raider, Raphael Semmes), and on their far right, concealed at the edge of the trees, was the Valverde Battery, captured from the Yankees during the Confederate invasion of New Mexico in 1862 and first commanded by another future governor of Texas, Joseph Sayers, then an assistant adjutant in one of Green's cavalry regiments.

When the commander of the Union corps, General Franklin, saw the presumptuous Confederate skirmishers drawn up in a line on the prairie, he called forth the full strength of the Nineteenth Army Corps. First one division then another deployed in line, fully a mile wide each. With drums beating and flags fluttering, the thick blue lines, bayonets glinting in the morning light, moved across the prairie toward the planta-tion house and the waiting rebels. The gray Texans, awed by the force arrayed against them, began backing toward the fence, and it appeared that this would be just another small bump on the Federal highway to Texas. When the Union infantry came within range, however, the two Confederate bat-teries opened fire and swept the field. General Franklin answered by calling out his own artillery, and the engagement was joined. Before it was over, both sides exchanged about one hundred artillery rounds. Matching the Confederate Valverde Battery was an equally famous Union battery, Nims's 2d Massachusetts. The New Englanders of Nims's battery would become well acquainted with the Texans over the next few weeks.

The high point of the morning was a dramatic cavalry charge by the Texans against the Union right. Three regiments came crashing out of the tree line, firing and yelling as they galloped across the prairie. When the screaming Texans, firing their pistols and swinging their sabers, reached their ranks, two regiments of Massachusetts and New York infantry

Battle of Buzzard's Prairie, October 15, 1863

cracked under the shock, and some began to run toward the rear. Before the break could be exploited, Edmund J. Davis's Federal horsemen came up and charged into their fellow Texans on the prairie, ending the threat. Meanwhile, one section of Nims's battery was driving the rebels back toward the fence in front of the plantation house, and another section dropped a shell into the ammunition wagon of Semmes's Confederate battery. One gray gunner was blown apart, another decapitated, and confusion seized the Confederate line. "Their bombs bursted in our ranks, making frightful gaps," one Texan wrote. In this artillery duel, as in so many others during

the war, the Union gunners prevailed.

Still, the firing continued from the plantation and its out-buildings and from the tree line bordering Bayou Bourbeau. The two lines had reached a standoff. Finally, at mid-morning, more bugles and drums and more flags coming up from the Union rear signaled the arrival of the Westerners of the Thirteenth Corps. Pushing forward through the lines of the Easterners, the veterans of Arkansas Post, Champion Hill, and Vicksburg drew into line while their batteries threw even more iron into the rebel ranks. Now completely overawed, the Texas cavalry officers ordered their men from the prairie, picked up their wounded, and retreated north across Bayou Bourbeau. A Wisconsin soldier could not avoid the lesson: the Easterners "thought they had bushed a grizzley and daresent fotch him so they sent for the western boys." The Western regiments pushed right up to the bayou, where a sharp Texas ambush brought the pursuit to a halt.

The "battle" of Buzzard's Prairie was a small affair, and not much was accomplished on either side. Green's cavalry finally forced a fight out of the Federals, but the blue columns threw them back and prepared to press on toward Opelousas, about ten miles farther north.

If the Louisianians along the lower Teche thought they had suffered the worst hardships of this war, they should have con-sulted the civilians south of Opelousas. One colonel of the Thirteenth Corps was relieved of command for "failing to per-form his duty and prevent marauding in his command." Union General E.O.C. Ord was so frustrated with his Westerners that he even allowed the citizens of Vermilionville to organize patrols to protect "themselves, their families, and personal property against marauders and thieves, white or black."

The efforts of general officers to maintain discipline had limited success, however. A Connecticut infantry captain wrote, "We forage like the locusts of Revelation. It is pitiful to see how quickly a herd of noble cattle will be slaughtered. Our

Negro servants bring in pigs, sheep and fowls, whether we bid it or forbid it." Harris Beecher, a surgeon in the 114th New York Infantry regiment of the Nineteenth Corps, reported that "the planters in that neighborhood lost immense quantities of what soldiers regard as legitimate spoils, viz., pigs, chickens, potatoes and sugar." Describing the wagon trains leaving the Bourbeau for Opelousas, Beecher wrote that "the wagons were loaded to the bows with everything one could mention, from a coffee-mill to a darkey baby. Their live stock was equally varied. Dogs, cows, goats, Shetland ponies, roosters, and a tame bear, embraced a part of the collection. It almost equaled the sight Noah must have produced when he opened the doors of his ark."

Before leaving Chretien Point a few days later, Beecher's comrades made sure to plunder the house and grounds of everything of value. Farm animals, corn, wagons, fence rails, even the large kitchen stove from the plantation house went north with the Federals. "They took everything," the mistress of the house sighed. "They left only the land."

The lighthearted descriptions of foraging recorded in Yankee letters and diaries were echoed in more bitter language by the local residents and by the Texans hovering around them, some of whom had never seen such destruction before. Indeed, the wasted landscape gave added motivation to the Texans in Taylor's army to resist the blue tide before it could reach their own homes. One of Taylor's cavalrymen told a Texas newspaper that the enemy "has completely devastated this country. Burned all the fences, corn and cotton houses, destroyed all corn near his line of march and many women and children within his lines are said, now, to be almost in a starving condition. Let the people of Texas prepare to meet such a foe, and with us to assist, he shall never trample down our homes and completely devastate our country as they have this."

The men in Walker's infantry division agreed. One, a chronic complainer who frequently flirted with the idea of deserting and simply going home, was convinced now that he was needed in the ranks. "I had rather stay here [in Louisiana]," he wrote his wife, "than for the Federals to get into Texas. It makes my blood run cold to see how they have laid waste the country they have passed through."

Despite their anger, the outnumbered Confederates could do little but fall steadily back in the face of the force arrayed against them. By noon on October 21, Federal regiments marched into Opelousas and Barre's Landing (present-day Port Barre), seven miles to the east. Three days later, Federal cavalry swept seven miles north of Opelousas and occupied the rich little village of Washington, home to many large planters in the area. Just beyond were the outposts of Taylor's army.

General Taylor, now down from Alexandria to command in person, was unhappy about retreating before the forces of Nathaniel P. Banks, and he determined to punish the blue cavalry near Washington. Just north of the village, he posted his infantry in the drainage ditches of a sugar plantation, scattered skirmishers among the slave houses, concealed his artillery in the edge of a wood, and waited for the Federal cavalry to attack him. Captain Petty of the 17th Texas Infantry described the pending ambush to his wife:

> Citizens were flying by us to the rear. Our Cavalry were driving back all the cattle and other stock left by the Citizens in their flight to keep the feds from getting it. The sick, the halt, the maimed, the blind with the wagons were sent to the rear. The horns (brass band) were sent away and the musicians transposed into an infirmary corps to pack off the wounded. The guns were furnished, amunition inspected, cannons planted, sharp-shooters and skirmishers thrown forward, every officer and man at his post and on the lookout.

General Albert Lee's U.S. cavalry turned back to Washington and avoided the ambush, however. The Confederate infantry remained in the ditches all night and until noon the next day before giving up on the surprise. Taylor would have to wait for another day for a fight.

General Taylor still was not sure what the Federal army planned to do. He and Kirby Smith feared that the two Union corps, now under the overall command of General Franklin, would strike out to the west. The Confederate generals even had an idea how Franklin and Banks might supply their army in the barren prairies of western Louisiana—by running supply schooners up the numerous rivers and bayous that penetrated the prairies from the Gulf of Mexico, enabling Franklin

One of the most interesting features of the Texas Overland Expedition was the presence of six governors of Texas in the two armies. Five Confederate officers and one Federal colonel occupied the governor's mansion in Austin during or after the war. The first, Colonel Edward Clark of the 14th Texas Infantry in Walker's Division, had succeeded the great Sam Houston as governor when Houston was forced to resign the office during the secession crisis of 1861. After the war four veterans of the expedition served consecutively as chief executive of Texas. Perhaps the most colorful was Colonel Edmund J. Davis of the 1st (U.S.) Texas Cavalry. He would be elected as the state's first Republican governor during the controversial political storm of Reconstruction and serve from 1870 to 1874. Captain Richard Coke of the 15th Texas Infantry, wounded at the Battle of Bayou Bourbeau, would succeed Davis as governor and serve from 1874 to 1876. Following Coke in office was Colonel Richard B. Hubbard (1876–1879) of the 22d Texas Infantry, also in Walker's Division. Succeeding Coke was Oran M. Roberts (1879–1883), another colonel under Walker and commander of the infantry at Bayou Bourbeau. Finally, at the turn of the century, former captain Joseph D. Sayers of the famed Valverde Battery would occupy the governor's chair (1899–1903). At least two other Union officers on the Texas Overland Expedition (in addition to Davis) also served as governors of their own states. Major General Nathaniel P. Banks, commander of the Federal Department of the Gulf, was governor of Massachusetts (1858–1861), and Major General Cadwallader C. Washburn, commander of the Thirteenth Army Corps, would be elected governor of Wisconsin and serve from 1871 to 1873.

to hopscotch from one supply base to the next, all the way to Texas. In Taylor's words, "[Franklin] could entirely abandon one base as soon as another was reached." Taylor had his cavalry and spies watch the roads west from New Iberia, Vermilionville, and Opelousas, worrying that the Federals might dash westward before he could strike at them.

If Taylor was impatient with the seeming indecision of the Federal generals, so were the men in the Union army. "It seemed as though the Texas campaign had become very infirm," wrote one soldier. "Creeping along for a little time, with slow and tottering pace, it had nearly reached the end of its existence." Wags in the Union camp began posing an arithmetic problem: "If the army moved thirty-five miles in two weeks, how long will it take to march to Niblett's Bluff?"

Unfortunately for them, their generals had no answer. Still waiting for specific orders from General Banks about which way to attack Texas—west toward the Sabine or north toward Shreveport—Franklin settled down at Opelousas and Barre's Landing for ten more days, unwilling to take the initiative himself. He had requested definite orders, but General Banks had sent word as early as October 11 that he "had no special instruction for you beyond what will naturally occur to you, viz, to hold your position in that quarter, and ascertain as much concerning the country in your front and on your flanks as possible, and to keep these headquarters well informed of what may transpire, with such suggestions as may occur to you."

Instructions like those would have given a more aggressive fighter an opening to take the initiative himself. But Franklin, beset by the caution that had plagued him ever since his failure to advance at the Battle of Fredericksburg in Virginia eleven months earlier, was unwilling to risk his army. On October 23 he sent another wire to headquarters in New Orleans: "I cannot say in this dispatch what I intend to do. Shall be very glad to get definite instructions." Hearing no response, Franklin wired again the next afternoon: "I respectfully reiterate my request for definite instructions...." Four days passed, and still no orders from New Orleans.

Franklin's lack of aggressive spirit stemmed partly from his own personality and partly from his deteriorating supply line to New Orleans. The bayous and rivers on which he depended were unusually low, preventing expected waterborne supplies from reaching his men at Opelousas and Barre's Landing. Nor could he expect much in the way of forage from the countryside. The farms and fields in the area had been picked clean during General Banks's spring campaign, and picked again on this expedition. The longer his army stayed in one place, the worse the problem became. To complicate matters, Green's Confederate cavalry was prowling his flanks and rear, gobbling up stray foragers, and generally making life miserable for the Federal quartermaster and commissary officers. "The rebels hang around us so incessantly that we cannot send out to get Anything [to eat]," an Indiana colonel complained to his wife in early November. Finally, Taylor kept his army well away from the Federal infantry, prompting Franklin to wonder whether there was any use of pushing farther into the wilderness.

General Franklin finally got off dead center on October 26 when he suggested to headquarters that he take his army back south to New Iberia. "By taking that position I can get forage more easily, and the supply of provisions [from New Orleans] can be kept up." Besides, he said, a cross-country invasion from New Iberia, south of Vermilionville, would be easier to supply. He had already sent Federal cavalry out west of New Iberia to search for horses and good roads to Niblett's Bluff.

While Franklin waited near Barre's Landing for approval of his plan, he received a surprising dispatch from New Orleans. The message informed him that Banks was no longer at department headquarters in New Orleans—he had taken off on another naval expedition to plant the flag in Texas, this time on the Rio Grande, and he had left orders for Franklin to send a few of his regiments back down the Teche for ultimate transfer to the forces on the Mexican border. Becalmed by his own caution, left on his own hook by Banks, irritated by the unceasing pinpricks of the Confederate cavalry, and increasingly worried about his shaky communications, Franklin decided definitely now to retrace his steps to New Iberia in order to secure a more dependable supply line.

The slow creep of the Texas Overland Expedition had finally stopped altogether by late October. Perhaps falling back to Vermilionville and then New Iberia and regrouping for another go at Texas was the answer.

5
THE CONFEDERATES STALK

By the time General Franklin sent his adjutants and order-lies scurrying around headquarters near Barre's Landing to prepare for the move back toward New Iberia, his army's paper strength of 37,000 soldiers had declined to about 24,500 men present for duty at the point of the invasion—12,200 in the Thirteenth Corps, 9,000 in the Nineteenth Corps, and 3,300 in the cavalry. Various regiments (including Edmund J. Davis's 1st Texas Cavalry) had been sent down the Teche to join General Banks on his expedition to the Texas-Mexico border, others had been left behind to occupy the supply line to Brashear City and New Orleans, some Federal soldiers had been scooped up by Tom Green's Confederate cavalry, and the army's sick lists included the usual numbers of men not avail-able for duty. Still, Franklin's blue army was nearly three times as large as Richard Taylor's 8,400-man force a few miles to the north.

General Taylor had begun gathering his forces north of Washington as soon as he learned that Banks was preparing another invasion into the interior. Taylor ordered Walker's Texas infantry division to leave its camps near Alexandria and march south in late September. When the Federal army crossed the Vermilion River and occupied Vermilionville on October 10, Walker's men began preparing for a serious fight. On October 11 Taylor ordered Walker to "have all your surplus baggage and the wagons not actually needed and indispensable sent to a camp at some eligible point. ..." General Walker was also instructed to "hold your command in light marching condition and ready at a moment's warning to move toward the enemy, fully prepared for action." Like soldiers in every army in every war, Walker's infantrymen had hurried to their destination and then—nothing happened. So they waited. They waited while Taylor tried to discern Federal intentions (and Franklin tried to divine Banks's plans).

During their stay in the sugarcane and Cajun country of south Louisiana, some of these Texans were as awed by the lush countryside as their northern counterparts. Captain Elijah Petty of the 17th Texas Infantry, writing home to his daughter from north of Washington, exclaimed that this "is the finest & richest country I have ever seen. It looks like the garden spot of the world." Another soldier in the division agreed: "The whole country through here is the richest I ever saw. Its just one Sugar farm after another. In fact, the whole country is covered with them. Louisiana is undoubtedly the richest State in the Confederacy... They have trees here growing in almost every shape you can mention. Some in the shape of large rocking chairs, others in the shape of tables ... Oh, I tell you, they are beyond discription."

Like their enemies in blue, the Texans also noted the wasting effects of war. Captain Petty described fields overgrown with weeds, deserted homes, and burned bridges. A former schoolteacher from Grayson County in north Texas, David Ray of the 16th Texas Cavalry (dismounted), described the rich farm country in a letter to his mother, but he noted that Louisiana's civilians suffered in the presence of any army, friend or foe: "very few of the plantations are cultivated and the homes are entered by the soldiers and every thing of value carried off that they want." Virgil Rabb of central Texas admitted the same to his own mother back in Fayette County: "The horrors of war are beyond description. There is nothing worse than a friendly army except the army of an enemy." Rabb then described how some of the men in his own division had entered an abandoned home and demolished a piano, apparently for the fun of it. "There is always men along in an Army mean enough to do almost anything in the world," Rabb concluded sadly.

While Taylor's army awaited further orders north of Washington, General Franklin finally began moving his columns back south toward Vermilionville on November 1. General Orders No. 22 instructed the army to begin moving at 6 A.M. All of the Nineteenth Corps and most of the Thirteenth would march as far as Carrion Crow Bayou, two miles south of the little fight at Buzzard's Prairie. The cavalry and one brigade of the Thirteenth Corps would hold the rear, three or four miles north of the rest of the army, "at their old camp ground" on Bayou Bourbeau. The old camp was a mile north of Buzzard's Prairie and about seven miles south of Opelousas. Wary of Green's cavalry, Franklin also ordered his officers to face their camps toward the rear, where trouble was most likely to develop. Franklin's disposition of his army on this step back toward Vermilionville gave Taylor what he had been seeking for the last month, an isolated portion of the blue army that he could attack with some chance of success. The lone Federal infantry brigade camped on the west bank of the Bourbeau now became Taylor's prey.

This unit was no ordinary prey, though. The 1,250 men in the five regiments of the brigade (the 60th and 67th Indiana, the 83d and 96th Ohio, and the 23d Wisconsin) were confident, tough, and experienced veterans. They had helped to turn Confederate invasions led by Edmund Kirby Smith and Braxton Bragg out of Kentucky in the fall of 1862, accompanied William Tecumseh Sherman on his failed and bloody mission to capture the bluffs at Chickasaw Bayou, borne the brunt of the fighting in the assault on Arkansas Post in early 1863, and accompanied Ulysses S. Grant through the battles of Port Gibson, Champion Hill, and Big Black River Bridge on the way to Vicksburg.

They had bled and died in the May 1863 attacks on Vicksburg's earthworks, and they had suffered through the long siege that followed. After Vicksburg surrendered, they had turned on the Mississippi capital at Jackson until it too fell under their control. Few brigades in the entire Union Army were as tough, as experienced, or as successful as this First Brigade of the Fourth Division of the Thirteenth Army Corps.

The commander of the brigade was Colonel Richard Owen, a fifty-three-year-old native of Scotland. The youngest son of Robert Owen, the famous British social reformer, and brother of Robert Dale Owen, the Indiana and New York reformer and Congressman, Colonel Owen was a man of some accomplishment himself. After his adventure on the Texas Overland Expedition, he would resign his commission and begin a long and distinguished academic career as a scientist on the faculty of Indiana University and first president of Purdue University.

Owen's role in the looming battle would be limited, however, because his division commander, Brigadier General Stephen Gano Burbridge, would handle the brigade himself when the shooting started. Burbridge, a native of Kentucky, a graduate of the Kentucky Military Institute, and a farmer and lawyer before the war, had seen considerable action before he ever came to Louisiana. He had fought at Shiloh, helped to capture Arkansas Post, and survived several engagements during the Vicksburg campaign. In the opinion of his admiring men, he was an officer worthy of the soldiers in the Thirteenth Army Corps.

Providing added strength to the Western infantry was Captain Charles Rice's 17th Ohio Battery of six ten-pounder Parrott guns, accurate and long-range field pieces. The gunners from Dayton had come to this bayou through the same storms as the foot soldiers under Burbridge and were well pre-

Stephen Gano Burbridge: born Kentucky 1831; attended Georgetown College and the Kentucky Military Institute, becoming a lawyer and plantation owner in Kentucky prior to the Civil War; a staunch Unionist in a state bitterly divided on the secession issue, he accepted a commission as colonel of the 26th Kentucky (US) Infantry; promoted to brigadier general, U.S. Volunteers, in June 1862, he com-

manded a brigade in the preliminary movements against Vicksburg later that year and was active in the Yazoo expedition, at Chickasaw Bluffs, and in the capture of Arkansas Post; he served credibly throughout the Vicksburg Campaign of 1863, after which he remained on duty in the Department of the Gulf; in April 1864 he assumed direction of the District of Kentucky, Department of the Ohio; brevetted major general of volunteers for his role in repulsing Confederate General John Hunt Morgan's celebrated raid in July 1864; despite this success, Burbridge quickly earned the hatred of most Kentuckians; an administrative demagogue, he routinely penalized citizens for the actions of Rebel guerrillas, compelled farmers and merchants to sell their produce and goods to the Federal government at below market value, and threatened to arrest anyone believed to oppose President Abraham Lincoln's re-election; to help cover these excesses and to bolster a sinking reputation, Burbridge launched an expedition against the vital Confederate salt mines in southwestern Virginia; in October 1864, after an order from General W.T. Sherman canceling the operation failed to reach him, Burbridge attacked a numerically inferior Confederate force at Saltville, Virginia, and was repulsed; this failure, coupled with his administrative abuses, prompted the general's removal in February 1865; his harsh wartime measures and the lingering animosity of Kentuckians prevented Burbridge from remaining in his native state following the war and forced the relocation of his family to New York. General Burbridge died at Brooklyn in 1894.

pared for combat. Supporting the infantry and artillery were about five hundred Federal horsemen under Colonel John G. Fonda, a skilled horseman from Warsaw, Illinois. Riding with Colonel Fonda's cavalrymen was one section of Nims's Massachusetts battery. All combined, about 1,800 Federal soldiers—infantry, artillery, and cavalry—pitched their tents along Bayou Bourbeau on November 1, faced north and west, and formed the rear of Franklin's southbound army. Their nearest support (the other regiments and brigades of the Thirteenth Corps) was about three and a half miles to the south, along Carrion Crow Bayou.

To the north of Burbridge's men hovered Green's Confederate horsemen, peering through their binoculars toward the Federal camp. At 4 A.M. on November 2, Green's cavalry scouts opened fire on Burbridge's outposts, sending an alarm through the Union camp and prompting the foot officers to roll their men out of their blankets to form a line on the prairie. This only robbed the westerners of their sleep, however, for the firing soon died away. The whole scene was repeated six hours later, again with no discernable results.

General Burbridge, nervous about his isolated position and uncertain about Green's intentions, decided finally to take the initiative. He put his infantry, cavalry, and artillery on the road leading north toward Opelousas, determined to learn just how many Confederates were out there and how eager they were for a fight. Before they had gone very far, they spied a large body of Texas cavalry out on the prairie. Burbridge's Parrott guns were rolled up, unlimbered, and prepared for action. The Confederate cavalry unlimbered their own field pieces, and the gunners in blue and gray commenced to throw shells across the prairie at each other for most of the day. In the end, Burbridge managed only to keep the rebels at arm's length for another day. Green, however, observed the whole Federal force—its components of different arms and its size. Now he and Richard Taylor knew what they needed to know—that the rear of Franklin's army was vulnerable.

That night, General Green sent a hurried note to Colonel Oran M. Roberts, senior commander of the three infantry regiments assigned by Taylor to support the cavalry: "The Genl Comdg directs that you report at his head quarters (the Catholic Church [in Opelousas]) with your whole command by daylight tomorrow morning. P.S. If Col Roberts has not come up dispatch a courier to him at once with orders to move up immediately."

Oran Milo Roberts: born South Carolina 1815; graduated from University of Alabama in 1836; studied law and was admitted to the bar in 1837; served a term in the Alabama Legislature; in 1841 moved to San Augustine, Texas, to practice law; appointed district attorney in 1844; district judge from 1846 to 1851; became president of the board of trustees and lecturer in law at University of San Augustine in 1845; associate justice of the Texas Supreme Court in 1857; a strong secessionist, he was unanimously elected president of the state Secession Convention in 1861; raised the 11th Texas Infantry and served as its colonel; in November 1863, while with Brigadier General Tom Green in Louisiana, led an attack on Federals at Bayou Bourbeau; Roberts reported: "Our whole line responded at once and rushed towards the enemy, and continued it through the enemy's camp, they having fled before us." In 1864, Roberts left the army to become chief justice of the Texas Supreme Court; removed from office when the war ended, he served as a member of the Constitutional Convention of 1866; elected by the Texas Legislature to the U.S. Senate, but was  denied his seat because of his Confederate activities; with the restoration of Democratic control in Texas, he returned to the Supreme Court until elected governor of Texas in 1878; upon his retirement in 1883, he became professor of law at the University of Texas; wrote several books and contributed to Dudley G. Wooten's *Comprehensive History of Texas* (1898) and Clement A. Evans' *Confederate Military History*, XI (1898). Roberts died in Austin in 1898.

St. Landry Catholic Church, occupied by Federal forces, October 1863

Roberts, colonel of the 11th Texas Infantry in Walker's Division, was a forty-eight-year-old lawyer and former justice of the Texas Supreme Court. A graduate of the University of Alabama, he had moved to Texas in 1841 and quickly established himself as one of the young republic's ablest attorneys. During the winter of 1860-61, he had been one of the most outspoken secessionists in the state, and he was unanimously elected president of the Texas secession convention. He backed up his rhetoric with action in early 1862 when he raised the 11th Texas Infantry Regiment, and he would serve as its colonel until 1864 when he became chief justice of the state Supreme Court. Fifteen years later he would be elected governor of the Lone Star State. As experienced as he was in the law, Roberts had no military training beyond his education as a cadet at the University of Alabama. His status as the senior colonel among the three regimental infantry commanders made him the acting commander of the temporary infantry brigade supporting Green's cavalry.

The three regiments under Roberts's control—his own 11th Texas, the 18th Texas of Walker's Division, and the 15th Texas, temporarily assigned to Walker—were camped on the northern outskirts of Washington, seven miles north of Opelousas, when Green's order reached him. Roberts's foot soldiers were enjoying some well-earned rest after two days of hard marching down Bayou Boeuf, but their officers roused them during the night and put them on the road to Opelousas. Just as dawn began to break on Tuesday, November 3, Roberts's men shuffled sleepily into the northern outskirts of Opelousas, found General Green's headquarters at the Catholic church, and flopped down on consecrated ground to cook their breakfast.

Of the three regiments, only one—the 15th Texas—had ever seen any action, even this late in the war. The 18th, in fact, was still armed with old-fashioned smoothbore muskets, effective only at distances under a hundred yards. The 950 men in Roberts's command were raw indeed to send against the well-armed and hardened veterans of Chickasaw Bayou, Arkansas Post, Champion Hill, and Vicksburg.

Two sections of artillery (two field pieces to a section) joined Green's 2,000 cavalrymen and Roberts's 950 foot soldiers that morning—one section of the Valverde Battery, battle-tested and experienced, and one from Captain James M. Daniel's Lamar Light Artillery. Daniel had been ill at home in Lamar County, Texas, for nearly a year, and his rifled section was commanded by Lieutenant James M. Hamilton. Normally assigned to Walker's Division, the Lamar Artillery was just as green in the ways of battle as most of Walker's infantry. The four field pieces in the artillery detachment were manned by fewer than a hundred men.

After breakfast on the church grounds, Roberts put his column on the road south out of Opelousas toward Bayou Bourbeau, seven miles away. Altogether, about 3,000 Confederates—cavalry, infantry, and artillery—were moving down the road. Now, all the tall Texas talk and bluster would be put to the test. This would be the first battle for most of the infantry. They were finally going "to see the elephant." Thoughts of home and family and religion doubtless crowded their excited minds as Walker's foot soldiers shuffled toward Franklin's Yankees.

Those who glanced over to the left of the road saw farm fields and, beyond the fields, a line of trees parallel to the road. The road and the tree line drew closer together the farther the men marched. To the right of the road were the open prairies of southwest Louisiana, not unlike those of central and north Texas, whence many of the infantrymen had come. And a few miles ahead was the enemy's camp.

While Colonel Roberts's Confederate foot soldiers were being rolled from their blankets in the middle of the night and put on the road toward Opelousas and Bayou Bourbeau, their counterparts in blue were up and stirring also. At 2 A.M. the Federal chief of pickets sent word to his outposts that the countersign had been changed; several Rhode Islanders had deserted during the night and probably given information to the enemy, so caution was paramount. Also at 2 A.M., General Burbridge, still nervous about Green's Confederate horsemen, called his five regimental commanders to his tent. By candlelight, Burbridge gave each regiment its orders for the day. By four o'clock the men of the entire brigade had been roused from their sleep and instructed to form a line on the prairie, facing north up the road to Opelousas and west toward the open prairie. The horsemen, Burbridge and his officers were convinced, would come at them from the prairie. There would be no need to place infantry in the woods bordering the bayou, to the right of the prairie, since the Texas cavalrymen preferred to inflict their torment out in the open, where they had room to maneuver.

Once they had stumbled into line in the early morning darkness, Burbridge's infantry went through a routine they had perfected by now. Surgeon J. T. Woods of the 96th Ohio could hear more than he could see:

> Then followed quickly the sounds of busy preparation. Everywhere was heard the click, click, of the rising hammer, and then the sharp explosion of the cap, by which it was known that the tube was open; and the clear ring of the rammer, as it was dropped into the barrel, satisfied its owner that he could rely upon his musket to do faithful execution in the moment of need. Cartridge boxes were carefully packed with 40 rounds, and canteens filled with water, that might quench the thirst of a dying comrade.

Colonel John G. Fonda's cavalry brigade was equally alert that Tuesday morning. His troopers were ready for another go at the rebel cavalry and his horses were saddled, all by 4 A.M.

Green and Roberts would not catch these veterans unprepared.

The Federals waited in the early morning coolness, but as
so often happens, nothing happened. Green's cavalry and
Roberts's infantry were still in the vicinity of Opelousas, seven
miles away. By 6 A.M. General Burbridge relaxed and allowed
his soldiers to return to camp for breakfast. For the rest of the
morning, while Taylor's Confederates were closing in from the
north, the Federals near the bayou busied themselves with
various tasks. Part of the cavalry brigade was assigned to
guard a forage train bound for the village of Grand Coteau, a
mile or so to the east. Other horsemen ventured a mile in the
opposite direction and bumped into Green's pickets, where-
upon a two-gun section of the 17th Ohio Battery rolled out
onto the prairie and resumed the previous day's long-range
shelling. Colonel Fonda followed the half-hour of artillery fire
with a deeper reconnaissance of about two miles, but by then
the Confederates had vanished as usual. By 10 A.M. Fonda's
cavalry was back in camp.

After breakfast the infantrymen returned to their line on
the prairie. But as the morning hours passed, some companies
of the 23d Wisconsin returned to camp in the rear to vote in
their state's elections and receive their pay from a Wisconsin
paymaster. Parts of other regiments were also allowed to go to
the rear and receive their pay. As noon approached, some of
the men were given permission to return to camp, shake out
their cooking utensils, and prepare the midday meal.

Shortly before noon, Colonel Roberts's slowly advancing
skirmishers were spotted by their Federal counterparts, and
the latter began throwing long-range rifle balls up the dirt
road toward the Texans. General Green then rode up to Colonel
Roberts and gave the foot soldiers their orders. They were to
file off the road to the left and form a line of battle. The line
would stretch about three-quarters of a mile, from the road,
through the farm fields, through the woods, to the banks of the

bayou. Green's horsemen would connect to the infantry at the road and then stretch to the right in a wide arc to the west and south across the prairie. The cavalry regiments on the extreme right of the Confederate line, commanded by Colonel James P. Major, would, according to the plan, sweep in behind the Federal left and roll up the blue regiments. The infantry,

James P. Major: born Missouri 1836; graduated from the U.S. Military Academy in 1856, twenty-third in his class of forty-nine; as 2d lieutenant, he joined the 2d U.S. Cavalry in Texas, where he served as adjutant to Major Earl Van Dorn and saw action against Indians; resigned his commission in 1861 to enter Confederate service; after serving on now Confederate General Van Dorn's staff, Major joined Sterling Price's Missouri state troops as a lieutenant colonel and led a cavalry unit at Wilson's Creek, Missouri, in August 1861; rejoined Van Dorn in Arkansas and

accompanied his mentor to Mississippi as chief of artillery; following Van Dorn's assassination in May 1863, Major moved to the Trans-Mississippi; promoted to colonel, he was given a cavalry brigade in General Richard Taylor's command in Louisiana; joined his brother-in-law General Thomas Green in opposing Federal movements in southern Louisiana; highly impressed, Taylor recommended Major's promotion to brigadier general; so promoted in July 1863, Major was sent with Green's command to the Texas coast to face a threatened Federal invasion, but quickly returned to Louisiana in response to General N.P. Banks's push up the Red River; fought well at Mansfield and Pleasant Hill; dispatched to harass the Federal flotilla during its retreat down the Red, he was present at Blair's Landing when Green was killed; when General John A. Wharton succeeded Green, Major's brigade formed part of Wharton's Division, passing the remainder of the war in Louisiana and Arkansas; following the war, he lived for a time in France before returning to the United States; engaged in planting in Texas and Louisiana; his second wife was the sister of Confederate General Paul O. Hebert; General Major died at Austin, Texas, in 1877. Major was a competent officer who constantly drew the praise of his superiors.

Arthur P. Bagby: born Alabama 1833, the son of Alabama senator and governor Arthur Pendleton Bagby and his second wife, Anne Connell; graduated from the U.S. Military Academy in 1852, thirty-sixth in his class of forty-three; brevet 2d lieutenant, 8th Infantry, 1852 to 1853; resigned to study law; practiced law in Mobile from 1855 until 1858 when he moved to Gonzales, Texas, where he practiced until appointed major of the 7th Regiment of Texas Mounted Volunteers in 1861; promoted to lieutenant colonel in April 1862 and to full colonel in November 1862; after participating in the unsuccessful invasion of New Mexico and clearing himself on a charge of drunkenness on duty, he led the 7th Texas in the recapture of Galveston in 1863, commanding a detachment of volunteers on a "cottonclad" gunboat; sent to Louisiana as part of General Henry Sibley's (later Thomas Green's) Texas cavalry, Bagby commanded his unit at the Battle of Berwick Bay in April 1863 where he received a wound in the arm but remained on the field until the Federals retreated; upon the promotion of Green to divisional command, Bagby led the Sibley-Green Brigade at the Battles of Fordoche and Bayou Bourbeau; during the Red River Campaign of 1864, Bagby engaged in rear guard actions against the Federal advance; on April 8 at the Battle of Mansfield, his dismounted brigade helped turn the Union right flank; during the Battle of Pleasant Hill on April 9, the brigade, again dismounted, captured an advanced Union position; thereafter, Bagby's calvary harassed the Federal retreat to Simmesport. General E. Kirby Smith, who earlier had recommended Bagby for promotion, assigned the "brilliant" Bagby to duty as brigadier general on April 13, 1864, to date from March 17; later given command of the 4th Brigade, 2d Cavalry Division, Bagby received permanent command of an entire cavalry division and on May 16, 1865, Kirby Smith promoted him to major general (to rank from May 10), but by then the war had ended. After the peace, Bagby resumed his law career in Victoria, Texas, and from 1870 to 1871 served as assistant editor of the Victoria *Advocate*; in the 1870s he settled in Halletsville, Texas, and established a successful law practice; Bagby, a "learned and a fine orator," continued as an active and prominent lawyer. He died in Halletsville on February 21, 1921, and is buried in the city cemetery.

advancing through the woods and corn fields on the extreme left, would come up behind the Federal right, still out on the prairie. The center of the rebel line, manned by Colonel A. P. Bagby's cavalry brigade and the two sections of artillery, would, it was hoped, distract Burbridge's officers long enough to allow the wings to do their work.

Roberts arranged his three regiments to conceal their weaknesses as much as possible. The 15th Texas, the only one with any battle experience, was placed on the infantry's right, anchored to the Opelousas road. It would link up to the cavalry and be most exposed to enemy fire during the advance. Roberts's own 11th Texas was sent to the far left, where the bayou snaked through the woods. The men of the 18th Texas, shouldering their old .69-caliber smoothbores, were nestled in the center of the infantry line where they would have the near-by advantage of the 15th's experience and the longer-range rifles carried by some companies of the 11th.

"The cornstocks and weeds [in the farm fields] served considerably to conceal from view our numbers," Roberts reported later. "By the time our skirmishers had advanced three hundred yards through the fields they commenced a brisk fire on each side of the road, which was returned by those of the enemy." Roberts, moving forward with his men, remained on his horse throughout the advance, the only infantry officer to do so. He had planned to return to Texas a few days earlier to recuperate from a nagging illness, but the opportunity to strike at the Yankees was too good to miss, especially for the chairman of the Texas secession convention.

The soldiers on the far left, the men of the 11th Texas, had to scramble to keep up with their comrades. The bayou on their left twisted and meandered through the woods, forcing the Texans to splash into the muddy water and cross to the other side to stay in line. Then a bit farther along, they had to jump in again when the bayou bent back around in the other direction. By the time they neared the Union line, some companies of the 11th decided simply to fall back a bit behind the 18th Texas rather than cross the bayou again. As a result, the neat ranks that Roberts and Green had envisioned were folded and doubled around each other, creating a thick mass of soldiers in the center of the Confederate infantry line.

Although they were not required to push back and forth through the waist-high water of the bayou, the men in the 18th and 15th Texas had their own problems. A thick bois d'arc (Osage orange) hedge in their path forced them to break their line, find narrow passages through the foliage, and then reform on the other side. The woods along the bayou were not an ideal setting for an infantry advance, either. The Texans had to climb over logs, push their way through vines and briars and thick underbrush, and leap over small ravines on their way to find the Yankees. The symmetry of their original line inevitably deteriorated, but on they pushed for a mile and a half before stopping for a few minutes' rest in a ravine, only five hundred yards from the Federal camp.

While Roberts's infantry moved ever closer to their unprotected right flank, Burbridge's unwary Federal regiments went about their morning tasks. Some companies of the 23d Wisconsin were voting and receiving their pay in camp, the 67th Indiana was also lining up to be paid and cooking the midday meal, and the 83d Ohio had left the scene entirely, assigned to a forage train bound for Grand Coteau on the other side of Bayou Bourbeau. Their officers had heard the skirmishing up the Opelousas road, but that was nothing new. Scattered firing by skirmishers had been standard fare throughout this campaign, and no one paid much attention to it. "During all this time, and until the final clinch," a Wisconsin officer wrote, "we all supposed it to be a mere guerrilla annoyance, that no serious attack was contemplated—and felt quite as safe as if in the streets of Madison."

6

THE BATTLE OF BAYOU BOURBEAU

While the men in Burbridge's brigade voted and cooked their meals and received their pay, several hundred yards north of the Federal camp, Roberts's infantrymen were taking their final rest before the coming storm. The two days of marching down Bayou Boeuf to Washington, the predawn jaunt from there to Opelousas, and the push through the woods and cornfields near the bayou had left Roberts's men fatigued. In a small ravine the men passed around canteens of water—the midday sun had warmed the air considerably—and relaxed for a few minutes while their officers made arrangements for the final push. Colonel Roberts replaced his exhausted skirmishers with fresher men, captains mingled with their companies, and all the while Minie balls from Federal skirmishers whistled nearby.

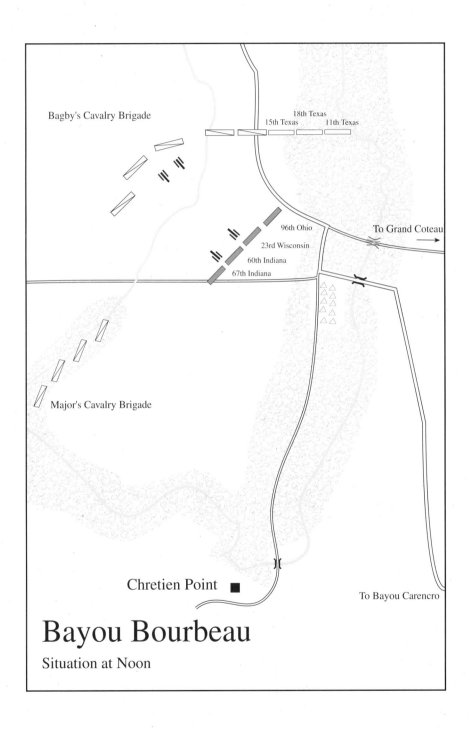

Bagby's Cavalry Brigade

18th Texas
15th Texas   11th Texas

96th Ohio

23rd Wisconsin

60th Indiana

67th Indiana

To Grand Coteau

Major's Cavalry Brigade

Chretien Point

To Bayou Carencro

Bayou Bourbeau

Situation at Noon

Captain Joshua Halbert of the 15th Texas, a lawyer from Corsicana in central Texas, was doubtless representative of many of the men in the ravine. "While we [were] resting the last time before we began to return the fire," he wrote his wife, "I thought of you and our darling little ones." Mental visions of wives and children were interrupted after ten minutes with the sharp order to "Charge—double quick!" and Halbert and the other Texans picked themselves up, adjusted their hats, checked their muskets and rifles one last time, and moved through the trees toward the Yankees.

The advancing Confederate foot soldiers were wedging in behind the Federal infantry on the prairie. General Burbridge's certainty that he would face only Green's cavalry on the prairie had led him to leave his right in the air, and Robert's Confederates were moving ever nearer the Federal camp at the rear of the blue infantry and artillery. "Up to this time," reported Colonel Joshua Guppey of the 23d Wisconsin, "no one supposed that the enemy had any infantry within striking distance of us.

...I think we could have driven the cavalry if it had been unaided by infantry." And yet, there they were, rushing forward through the woods and threatening to completely overlap the right end of the blue line.

By this time, the increasing volume of noise and smoke in the woods had attracted the notice of Union officers in camp and on the prairie. This did not sound like the usual skirmishing with Green's cavalry—and it was coming from the woods, where no one had expected trouble. Some of the officers, including General Burbridge, finally realized what was happening and began shouting orders for the men cooking their meals and receiving their pay to rush back to their companies and regiments and prepare for action. Reuben Scott of the 67th Indiana was one of those still in camp to receive his pay. "Suddenly we heard the pickets firing off in the front," he remembered, "and thinking we had another day's skirmishing on our hands we, without putting on our coats, buckled on our cartridge boxes and grabbed our faithful rifles, and were in ranks in a few minutes and moving out by flank to meet the enemy while the paymaster flew to the main army [on Carrion Crow Bayou], some four miles away."

As squads and companies ran forward to join their regiments, General Burbridge galloped back and forth along his line, waving his hat and shouting orders to his officers. His force, before he began making adjustments to meet the threat in the woods, included the 67th Indiana on the far left, then the 60th Indiana, the 23d Wisconsin, and the 96th Ohio on the right near the Opelousas road. One section of the 17th Ohio Battery and one of Nims's 2d Massachusetts Battery were already unlimbered in front of the two Indiana regiments and firing toward the woods on the right. The fifth regiment in the brigade (the 83d Ohio) was already across the bayou on its foraging expedition. Colonel Fonda took his cavalry across the bayou also, hoping to recross from east to west behind the advancing gray infantry and gobble them up as they retreated, as surely they must, before the veterans of Vicksburg.

Burbridge was fully aware now that his brigade was in danger of being enveloped, and he rode from regiment to regiment, ordering his colonels to move to the woods on the right. The 60th Indiana was quick to recover from the surprise and dashed over toward the trees, taking position in advance of the 96th Ohio. Now came the 23d Wisconsin, also sliding to the right and falling in near the Ohioans. By this time Roberts's Confederates were in full contact with the Federal infantry in the woods. "Our boys poured a murderous fire on them along the whole line," a Texan in the 15th remembered. The gun smoke filling the space between the tree tops and the ground occasionally obscured the two lines from each other, and the awful clatter of battle smothered the voices of their officers, but the men on both sides continued to fire, reload, and fire again.

Captain Richard Coke of the 15th Texas, another future governor of the Lone Star State, fell with a wound in his chest near the Opelousas Road. Private P. Alonzo of the same regiment felt a jolt against his rifle and was horrified to see that his trigger finger had been shot away. A Private Story of Company G doubled over screaming when a Minie ball ripped through his scrotum. At the opposite end of Roberts's line, Captain J. L. H. Stillwell of the 11th Texas was wounded twice, in the left buttock and right thigh, and he died four days later. Not far away, Private Wimberly of the 11th gushed blood when a ball zipped through his throat. Somehow, he managed to live three more days. Christopher Koonce of Company A, hit in the leg, survived, but he lost his leg to the surgeon's saw after the battle.

The soldiers of the 18th Texas were falling too. Private J.

Richard Coke: born Virginia 1829; after graduating from William and Mary College in 1849, he studied law and was admitted to the bar in 1850; before the Civil War, he moved to Waco, Texas, where he practiced law; in 1852 he married Mary Horne of Waco; they had four children; Coke entered Confederate service as a private in 1861 and served throughout the war, rising to the rank of captain; appointed a district judge in 1865 and elected judge of the Texas Supreme Court in 1866, he was removed from the bench in 1867 by General Philip Sheridan as "an impediment to reconstruction"; in 1873 Coke defeated Edmund J. Davis in a dramatic gubernatorial campaign which, after the affair known as the Coke-Davis Controversy, restored Democratic rule and marked the political end of Reconstruction in Texas; Coke was re-elected in 1876 and served until 1877, when he resigned to become a U.S. senator; he served in the Senate from 1877 to 1885; he died in Waco in 1897 and was buried in Oakwood Cemetery.

M. Elkins's elbow was split open; he, too, would spend the rest of his life with an amputated limb. Corporal E. Willingham had part of his face torn away. Private Jesse Steelman of Company H somehow survived a head wound from a shell thrown into the woods by the Federal artillery. Colonel Roberts himself was thrown to the ground when a Yankee bullet dropped his horse, but the secessionist judge regained his feet and urged his regiments forward.

Across the space between the two lines, Federal soldiers, too, were falling. A nineteen-year-old farm boy from southern Wisconsin was hit in the face and killed on the spot. Corporal Charles McGarvey of the 60th Indiana was struck by three balls at almost the same moment. Sergeant Henry Endicott of the 60th dropped to the forest floor when a ball speared him in the left eye. Charles Stanfield from Ohio was hit in the chest. When his regimental surgeon reached his side, the doctor heard him whisper one last call to his mother.

Federal officers in the woods found it almost impossible to prevent their men from backing away from the enemy, who seemed to spill out through the trees, bayonets pointing forward, in ever larger numbers. The real problem was that Northern regiments were arriving on the scene one at a time, and they could not withstand the pressure from the more numerous Texans.

First the 60th Indiana broke and ran back through the ranks of the 96th Ohio. That created confusion among the Ohioans, and they too began to crack and fall back through the trees into the line of the 23d Wisconsin. Colonel Guppey of the 23d was rushing back and forth, trying to rally the retreating Indianans and Ohioans, and sending hurried appeals to General Burbridge to send reinforcements to the woods. Burbridge had already thought of that and sent an order to the 67th Indiana, still on the prairie near the artillery, to slide right and shore up the crumbling blue infantry. The general was frustrated when the 67th did not move, so he sent a sec-

Attack on the 60th Indiana

ond messenger to Lieutenant Colonel Theodore Buehler of the 67th, ordering him to take his men to the woods. After a few minutes without a response, Burbridge sent a third orderly to the Prussian colonel with instructions to move instantly. It was too late, however. By this time, Buehler's 67th was being over-whelmed by Bagby's charging Confederate horsemen, and the 67th never did join the fight in the woods.

The situation on the Union right now depended on the only regiment still under firm control, Colonel Guppey's 23d Wisconsin. The 67th Indiana was busy on the prairie, the 83d Ohio was hurrying back from its foraging assignment, and the 60th Indiana and 96th Ohio were rushing backward past Guppey. "It was about this time," Guppey reported, "that General Burbridge, waving his hat as he dashed up, ordered me to take position in a ravine between the right of the camp and the bayou." Guppey moved his regiment to the ravine and ordered his men to lie down, thus allowing the fleeing 60th Indiana and 96th Ohio to rush over them. Colonel A. H. Brown of the 96th Ohio joined with Guppey and rallied some of his men in the ravine with the Wisconsin regiment.

Guppey ordered his Federals to wait, to hold their fire until Roberts's onrushing rebels were "within good rifle-range." His regiment did not have to wait long; within a few minutes they sighted the Confederates, yelling their high-pitched shriek and firing as they came through the trees straight toward the ravine. Guppey noticed that the rebel line seemed disorga-nized. "The regiment in my front [the 18th Texas] was so dou-bled up that its men were 10 or 12 deep, and all mixed up, but still gallantly advancing."

What the Wisconsin colonel saw, no doubt, was partly the result of the confusion and excitement of battle, of the inevitable breakdown of neat lines in the woods, and of the men of the 11th Texas having fallen in behind the 18th to avoid crossing and recrossing the bayou. No matter the explanation, the result was that the Confederates had considerably more infantry—and momentum—at the point of contact than Guppey had to resist them.

When the 18th Texas approached within about eighty yards of the ravine (close enough for their smoothbores to take effect), the Confederates loosed a terrific volley that took down about forty of Guppey's men. At that moment Guppey himself was wounded below his left knee, the Confederate cavalry came sweeping in behind the Union left, and the whole Federal line began to crumble. Indianans and Ohioans, now joined by the men from Wisconsin, turned away from the rebel horde and headed for the rear. Back they ran, out of the ravine, through the woods, and through their camp toward safety on the other side of Bayou Bourbeau. And Roberts's Confederates were on their heels.

The Confederate infantry had been engaged for a full half-hour before the cavalry on the prairie advanced into the fray. Two of Colonel Bagby's regiments, dismounted for the fight, and the two sections of artillery that had come from Opelousas moved up within four hundred yards of Burbridge's center. There, two sections of Federal field pieces were alternating fire between the woods to their right and the cavalry on the prairie. Providing cover for the Union guns was the 67th Indiana Infantry, now formed into a hollow square to receive the coming cavalry charge.

After the Valverde section fired a few rounds toward the blue line, Bagby's cavalry (mounted and dismounted) began a general advance across the prairie. While the Union defenders were preoccupied with the Confederates in their front and in the woods to the right, on their far left Major's cavalry brigade spurred their horses forward and began one of those wild, mad dashes that cavalrymen loved so well, whooping, hollering, and waving their sabers and pistols as they galloped toward the left rear of the Federal line. One of Major's troopers described the scene: "Look across the smoothe prairie without a bush or ravine for cover, comes [Major's] charging column.

Capture of the 67th Indiana

...The air is full of grape, canister, shells and minnie balls. We near the battery—the enemy give way—the gunners leave their pieces—the battery and its infantry supports surrender—they are ours!"

Surgeon Woods of the 96th Ohio, watching the combat from near the camp, described the events from the Federal perspective: "The fierce cavalry sweep like a whirlwind among [the guns] with gleaming sabers. The swift riders enfold them and, almost without resistance, march them away captive before our eyes." A corporal in the beleaguered 67th Indiana still had vivid memories of the scene thirty years later: "Both forces become all mixed, and a pandemonium of sticking with bayonets, clubbing of muskets and shooting with revolvers. Meanwhile a storm of grape and cannister was pouring into this fighting mass from front and rear, while a cloud of smoke is spread over the scene."

George Chittenden, an officer in the 67th Indiana, described the disaster in a letter to his wife two days later.

> They came sweeping over the prairie like an avalanche. Our brave fellows met them however like [noble?] Greeks, and a most terrible hand to hand conflict ensued, in our own camps. Gen Burbridge pushed up and down the lines shouting to the brave boys who had followed him so long, not to fall back an inch....Gen Burbridge moved one cannon himself and worked it with terrible effect until the enemy were all around the guns, and some of their horses jumping over them, when our artillery men took their gun rammers and knocked rebs off their horses and drove them away. But the enemys name was legion, and the odds was too great.

For all the gunpowder burned on both sides in this charge—and all the florid language in postwar memoirs—relatively few men in either line were wounded and only one was killed. Lieutenant Colonel Buehler and most of his 67th Indiana were captured, three of the four Federal guns were temporarily disabled, and the center and left of the Union line evaporated. Thus, for the second time in the war, the 67th Indiana was captured by the enemy. Only a year earlier, the hapless Hoosiers had been bagged by Braxton Bragg during his Confederate invasion of Kentucky. A few months after the Battle of Bayou Bourbeau, Colonel Buehler was exchanged, court-martialed for cowardice and incompetence, and dismissed from the army. All his appeals to President Lincoln were rejected, and the disgraced officer took his place as the scapegoat for the disaster on the Bourbeau.

Into the smoke and noise and confusion in the woods and on the prairie arrived the fifth regiment of the Federal brigade, the 83d Ohio. They abandoned their foraging and raced back to camp just as the Union infantry came streaming out of the ravine in wild retreat. While their comrades ran past them toward the bayou, the 83d was met by General Burbridge and ordered to the western edge of the battlefield to support the remnants of the artillery and 67th Indiana. The Ohio men momentarily checked the gray cavalry's advance, but they too were soon thrown back toward the bayou. "In the end," one soldier in the 83d wrote, "our men were outnumbered so much, they had to run for dear life through the camp, leaving everything behind, the enemy cutting down the wounded with their sabres. Tom said he made one fellow toter in his saddle who had buried his sword in the head of one of [our] company, after throwing up his hands for mercy. These Texans are very blood thirsty in the heat of battle."

The camp in the rear of the original Federal line was now a maelstrom of confusion. Union infantrymen intermingled with cannoneers, newspaper reporters, black cooks and teamsters, and numerous slaves who had fled to supposed safety with the Federal soldiers—all rushing toward the bayou while a few officers tried to reestablish a line. But it was too late. The cavalry were riding among them, cutting some down, knocking over others with their horses, firing their pistols, and spreading general panic.

Surgeon Woods of the 96th Ohio crossed the bayou just ahead of the infantry. He described the attempts of Union teamsters to escape with what few supplies they could bring off the field: "In mad haste some dashed into the deep ravine, to find their wagons instantly mired. Others, with more coolness took their places, rapidly flew over the bridge, and, with lavish whip and spur, escaped." Not far behind Woods was Isaac Jackson of Ohio. "Now every man (after we got in the woods) ran and fought for himself. The rout was in earnest," Jackson remembered. "I ran until I got through the woods [on the other side of the bayou] when I caught hold of the spare wheel of a caisson and drug along for several yards on the ground, when I managed to get on top."

While some of the gray cavalry plunged into the woods, across the bridge and bayou, and emerged onto the eastern prairie in pursuit of the fleeing Federals, others stopped in the Union camp, awed by the rich spoils of war, and proceeded to grab everything they could carry with them—food, clothes, money, rifles, cooking utensils, whatever was available. Long accustomed to a meager diet and ragged clothing, they could not resist the temptation. Indeed, the undisciplined cavalrymen were so engrossed in pillaging Union tents and knapsacks that they momentarily ignored the Federal soldiers still streaming through them toward the bayou.

First Lieutenant William Marland, 2d Massachusetts Battery, earned the Congressional Medal of Honor for his heroic dash across the bridge over Bayou Bourbeau

At this point, First Lieutenant William Marland of Nims's Massachusetts Battery earned the Congressional Medal of Honor. Seeing no infantry left to support him but plenty of excited Confederates between him and the bridge over Bayou Bourbeau, he limbered his two guns, ordered his cannoneers to draw their pistols, and charged directly through the cavalrymen roaming through the Union camp. Firing as they went, his section rumbled at full gallop through the camp and toward the bayou, only to discover that the bridge across the muddy stream was crowded now with Roberts's gray infantry. In Marland's cool words, "it was necessary to charge through, which was accomplished without loss." A few Confederates did lose their dignity, flying over the bridge railing into the muddy water to avoid the fleeing New England limbers and guns.

The Federal artillery escape was only partially successful, however. Green's horsemen caught up to one of the Ohio guns near the bayou and killed its horses. "The moment it stopped the Rebs were thick around it," an Ohio soldier wrote. "I was verry sorry to see them around it, but I couldn't help it." He preferred to return to Ohio without a side trip to a Rebel prison camp.

Artist's depiction of William Marland's charge

The Confederate infantry, having pushed the Federals back into their camp and across the bayou, were still busy while the cavalry were gobbling up Federal prisoners and knapsacks. Almost as soon as they had broken the Union line, Colonel Roberts turned his men about face and started them back through the woods they had just fought through. Danger was in their rear.

Colonel Fonda's Federal cavalry had remained east of the bayou during the hardest part of the fight and then crossed another bridge to the rear of Roberts's men as they pushed south toward the Union line, hoping to capture the Texans if they retreated. Roberts, preoccupied with the advance, had sent one company of his 11th Texas to block Fonda's horsemen. Even with the aid of a gray cavalry regiment, the infantry company had not managed to disperse the Federal cavalry in the rear, however. Roberts had been unable to do much about all this while his men were engaged so closely with the Union infantry in front, but now he led his regiments back to dispose of the threat. Within a few minutes, the Confederates had scattered and chased Fonda's horsemen back across the bayou and even rescued a few of their men taken prisoner earlier.

With the rear secure, Roberts reversed his march once again, moved back to the Union camp, and provided support for Green's artillery, which had moved forward to shell the retreating Federals on their way south. Those among Green's cavalry who were more disciplined (that is, not looting Federal tents) and those who were in the hottest pursuit galloped into the woods, across the bridge, and onto the prairie east of the bayou to finish off the remnants of Burbridge's Brigade.

The paymaster of the 23d Wisconsin, who had thrown his cash boxes and papers into a wagon and rushed toward the rear when the battle erupted, was one of those racing for safety. "The prairie was a moving spectacle of teams and stragglers, going at the highest speed," he reported. "On our left hand, about a hundred rods distant, stood a huddle of soldiery

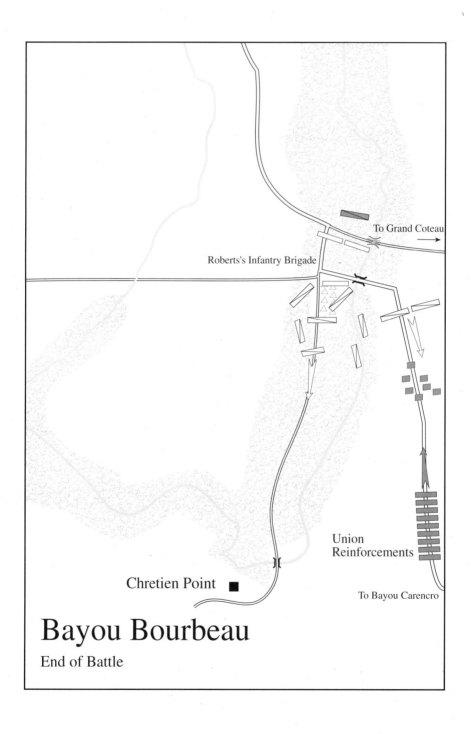

To Grand Coteau

Roberts's Infantry Brigade

Union
Reinforcements

Chretien Point

To Bayou Carencro

Bayou Bourbeau

End of Battle

in apparent disorganization —the debris of the brigade —all, indeed, that remained of it —about three hundred in number." The paymaster's wagon sped on toward safety on Bayou Carrion Crow, three miles to the south, but his heart dropped when he looked over his shoulder and saw Green's horsemen burst out of the tree line in pursuit. "When we saw that cloud break out of the woods into the field, it certainly looked as if the chances for going to Dixie were of the first class. It was the most exciting, not to say exhilarating, race I ever got caught in."

James R. Slack: born Pennsylvania 1818; educated at an academy in Newton, but at age nineteen moved to Indiana with his parents where he worked on a farm, taught school, studied law, and was admitted to the bar in 1840; a few weeks later, possessing only six dollars in cash and the clothes he was wearing, settled in Huntington, Indiana; elected county auditor in 1842, he held the position for nine years; after serving seven terms in the state senate, he was defeated for Congress

in 1854; commissioned colonel of the 47th Indiana Infantry in 1861, Slack commanded a brigade under John Pope at New Madrid and Island No. 10; after serving in district and post commands, he participated in the White River expedition and the engagement at Yazoo Pass; during the Vicksburg Campaign he commanded a brigade of McClernand's Thirteenth Corps; transferred to the Department of the Gulf, where he remained there throughout the remainder of the war, he played a minor part in the Red River Campaign; commanded a division of the Thirteenth Corps at Thibodeaux, Louisiana, for a time; participated in the operations against Mobile, including the capture of Spanish Fort, Fort Blakely, and the city itself; promoted to brigadier general of volunteers in 1864, and brevetted major general in 1865, he returned to his law practice in Huntington, Indiana, after the war; appointed by the governor to the new Twenty-eighth Judicial Circuit and then elected in 1872 and reelected in 1878, he again ran unsuccessfully for Congress in 1880; the following year, while visiting in Chicago, Slack died of a heart attack; he was buried in Mt. Hope Cemetery, Huntington.

Fortunately for the retreating soldiers and civilians, rein-forcements from Carrion Crow Bayou were already approach-ing. Two divisions of General Washburn's Thirteenth Corps had started toward the sound of the guns shortly before, and the leading brigades arrived just as Burbridge's men emerged from the woods. The colonel of one of the brigades coming up from the rear, James R. Slack of Indiana, was appalled at the scene east of the bayou:

> ...his [Burbridge's] wagon train came on the prairie in a perfect stampede, wagons filled with great healthy men with their guns in their hands, teams in a full run, negroes eyes nearly all white, looking back over their shoulders. I abused the cowardly pups as much as I had time and ability to do, but they took no offence at it. Our boys jeered them a great deal. It was a novel sight indeed.

Washburn's heavy infantry lines and fresh artillery brought Green's horsemen up short, and most of the fleeing wagons, soldiers, and civilians passed through Washburn's line to safety.

While nearly all the action in the battle took place in the woods and on the prairies bordering Bayou Bourbeau, a small-er affair was playing itself out near the Federal camp on Carrion Crow Bayou three miles to the south. One of Colonel Major's Confederate cavalry regiments had struck off behind the Union line, across Buzzard's Prairie, and toward the larger camp of the Thirteenth Corps to create whatever havoc they could in that direction. A few Federal regiments from Washburn's Third Division were still in camp guarding artillery and wagon trains and were quite unprepared to find the yelling Texans suddenly in their midst. The gray horsemen created momentary confusion and considerable excitement, but they were too few to take on the Union infantry in camp, and they soon withdrew, leaving one casualty behind.

Back on the Bourbeau, Green's guns near the Union camp and the Federal artillery east of the woods launched shells at each other for a while, but neither side inflicted much harm on the other. General Green, realizing that the odds were now against him, gathered up his wounded, his prisoners, and all the Union camp equipment that could be hauled away, burned the rest, and returned to Opelousas. The Battle of Bayou Bourbeau was over.

7
THE AFTERMATH

As the sound of scattered firing faded to the rear, Green's victorious little army tramped back up the Opelousas Road to their supply train on the south edge of the village. While the exhausted survivors of the battle flopped down and cooked their evening meals, ambulances rolled on to the middle of town, where the surgeons converted the courthouse into a temporary hospital.

The Texans were highly impressed by the women of Opelousas and the surrounding countryside, who came immediately to the aid of the wounded. "Young and old, Catholic and Protestant, [they] came crowding in, and waited upon our men just as if they had been their husbands and brothers," one private remarked. Captain Halbert of the 15th Texas, the Corsicana lawyer who had let his mind wander to his wife and children while waiting in the ravine just before the final charge, also admired the Louisiana women:

> On the evening [the wounded] were carried to
> town although it was night, these noble women
> hurried to the hospital with beds, blankets, lint
> etc etc, threw aside all false modesty stripped
> them, bathed and dressed their wounds, put them
> to bed, sat up by them during the night and
> nursed them with all the fondness of mothers.
> And such quantities of soups and other good
> things as they sent in next day you have not seen
> in a long time.

Seven miles to the south, the scene in the Federal camp
was gloomier. "The buildings near the bayou were filled with
wounded men...," a New York surgeon wrote. "Rows of dead
bodies were laid out upon the grass, which were being buried
as fast as graves could be dug." The surgeon of the 96th Ohio
Infantry, working nearby, remembered "ghastly pools of blood."
An Ohio foot soldier wandered up and observed the gory labor:
"Many of [the wounded were] lying on the ground in the last

**The Opelousas Courthouse was used as a prison and signal corps station
by Federal forces**

throes of agony, with no one paying any attention....The surgeons were going on, busy with their dreadful work of amputation. The bloody work, the groans of the wounded, the dead lying so still, covered with blood, Oh Susie, 'twas a dreadful sight...."

Even the survivors of the day's carnage had legitimate complaints. "Since the rebels had burned up all our tents and camp equipage, we were left here upon this bleak prairie without blankets, tents or food," a soldier of the broken 67th Indiana lamented. Even in the midst of suffering, though, some of the Western veterans could still find reason to smile. The Ohio soldier who had quavered at the sight of the surgeons' saws soon walked over to the campfires of the survivors and found an amusing scene. "It is really laughable to hear some of the boys bemoan the loss of their clothing, saying every once in a while, that some dirty rebel is strutting around in his parade suit, or while he is shivering by the fire, some rebel rascal is snug and warm wrapped in stolen blankets."

By the time officers on both sides filed their required reports, casualties from the Battle of Bayou Bourbeau had been counted and summarized in clean, neat columns. Green's Confederates lost 22 men killed (all but one in the infantry), 103 wounded (about three-fourths in the infantry), and 55 missing (41 of them in the infantry). Clearly, Colonel Roberts's foot soldiers had borne the brunt of the fighting, as his men were quick to point out. "Green's [Bagby's] and Major's cavalry brigades were both with us on the occasion, and did good service in taking prisoners after the infantry routed the enemy— but nothing more," Captain Halbert told his wife back in Texas. "They did no good in the fight." General Walker himself was not above a bit of boasting (and exaggeration) about his previously untested soldiers: "Confederate cavalry took but little part in the engagement save to bring in the prisoners when the rout became general."

Federal losses in killed and wounded were not much different from those among the Rebels—25 killed and 129 wounded—but the Yankees had lost more than ten times as many captured—562, including 30 commissioned officers. "Some regiments lost more than half their number," the New York Herald's correspondent reported. "The Sixtieth Indiana went in with two hundred and seven, and lost one hundred and twenty-one; and the Ninety-sixth Ohio went in with fewer, and lost one hundred and nineteen." In addition, of course, most of the 67th Indiana had been marched off as prisoners. In sum, of the 3,000 Confederates of all arms engaged on November 3, about 180 (6 percent) were eventually counted as casualties. Among the 1,800 Federals caught up in the fight, 716 (40 percent) were lost.

On the morning after the battle, the two sides observed a flag of truce and exchanged some of their wounded prisoners. (The Confederates refused to return officers.) The Federals had buried their dead the night before, and the Confederates near Opelousas were digging graves for their own that morning. During a lull in the proceedings on the battlefield, Captain Halbert of the 15th Texas Infantry and a few other Confederate officers accepted an invitation to lunch, extended by a major on General Washburn's staff. Halbert described the occasion in a letter to his wife:

> The Major (Morgan) having an ambulance full of good things had a cloth spread on the grass in the yard [of a house serving as a hospital], nice edibles—such as neither you or I are accustomed to getting these hard times—displayed thereon and invited us to participate with him. First however he proffered some splendid liquors (of which there was a great quantity) which being duly acknowledged (My wife knows her husband's failings) we ate bountifully of the repast and closed the treat with the finest segars, from them also,

that I have seen for more than two years. During
all this time a pleasant agreeable conversation
was going on, though we poor Confederates had
nothing to give them....

This strange picnic, spread out on the bloody hospital
ground, continued for two hours before the two groups of officers parted. "I ought to add that they had given every attention
to our wounded and when they turned them over to our surgeons sent along with them crackers, butter etc and some fine
liquors for stimulants," Halbert added. "It [the meeting] was
interesting to me both on account of its novelty (to me) and of
the good breeding and gentlemanly propriety of those who
meet thus."

Apparently, General Taylor's Confederate surgeons and officers had been equally kind to the Federal wounded; General
Washburn's official report mentioned that "all our prisoners
are well treated." How some men can maim each other at midday—all too common—and treat each other with compassion
hours later—all too rare—is one of the mysteries of warfare.
The best and worst of human nature swirled in concentrated
form around that picnic blanket.

On the second day after the battle, General Franklin
resumed his march south toward Vermilionville and New
Iberia. Many of his soldiers, especially in the Thirteenth Corps,
marched down the narrow roads complaining angrily about
their leaders. In their letters and diaries and in their postwar
reminiscences, many of the Westerners, accustomed to victory,
blamed their humiliation on Eastern generals. "The blame of
this disaster lies on Gen. Franklin's shoulders," wrote Isaac
Jackson, the lucky Ohioan who had escaped capture or worse
by grabbing onto the fifth wheel of a passing caisson. Frank
McGregor, a member of Jackson's regiment, agreed: "There
was poor generalship somewhere. Our boys neither like the
eastern troops or their Generals, having but little confidence

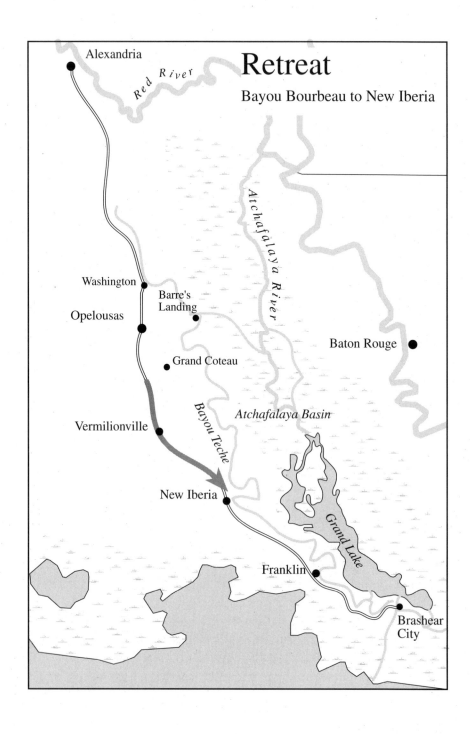

in Banks, Washburn or Franklin." Henry Watts of Indiana was embarrassed. "This was the first time the 13th Army Corps ever turned its back," he muttered.

Even some Easterners in the Nineteenth Corps expressed disgust. "If General Franklin is introducing the same plans and conducting this campaign in the same manner that the campaigns on the Potomac have been conducted I no longer wonder that they have failed so often," a Maine artillerist wrote to a friend. A correspondent of the *Boston Traveller*, writing from General Franklin's own headquarters, grumbled that "it was a shameful affair on our part." To Franklin's credit, he did not smooth the edges of the harsh truth. He admitted that his rear guard had been "severely handled" on the Bourbeau, and in a report filed three months later he called the whole affair "a discreditable surprise on our part."

The embarrassment gnawing at the Federals would doubtless have been exacerbated if they had understood that Green's force had numbered only 3,000 men. Officers and soldiers in the Thirteenth Corps and civilian observers traveling with them consistently overestimated Confederate strength at Bayou Bourbeau. General Burbridge reported the rebel force at 3,500 infantry and 2,500 cavalry and believed his was "an exceedingly moderate estimate." Colonel Guppey of the 23d Wisconsin believed Green's force included more than 5,000 men. The paymaster who had been paying Guppey's men and then raced to safety on the back of a wagon gave figures of 2,500 infantry and 4,000 cavalry. Isaac Jackson was sure he had seen "3,000 or 4,000 infantry and 3,000 cavalry," and the reporters for the *New York Herald* and *Washington National Intelligencer* put Green's force at 5,500 and 5,000, respectively.

Of course, the Confederates were certain that they had defeated a much larger force than Burbridge's 1,800 men. Tom Green believed he had whipped two brigades of Yankees, not one. General Taylor reported that his men had stampeded a whole division of Washburn's corps, about 4,000 men.

Likewise, General Walker boasted in his postwar memoir that his green infantry had manhandled an entire division of the Thirteenth Corps. The inflated estimates on both sides seem to be primarily the products of poor intelligence and "the fog of war," the inevitable confusion and misinformation that normally accompany battle. Still, it doubtless made the whole affair less humiliating (for the Federals) or more brilliant (for the Confederates) to believe that they had taken on twice as many of the enemy as they in fact had faced.

While the Federals grumbled and groused about the reverse at the Bourbeau, some of the more exuberant Confederates were congratulating themselves and exaggerating their accomplishment. An officer in General Green's headquarters wrote a Houston newspaper that the Confederates had "rout[ed] and scatter[ed] their boasted '13th Army Corps' to the four winds." In fact, he continued, "The men and their officers are confident that we can whip Gen. Franklin's entire force with the greatest ease." One of the Confederates who had conversed with the Federals under flag of truce the day after the battle was equally proud of besting the Westerners of the Thirteenth Corps. "They compliment our boys for their fighting qualities in very high terms," he wrote. "Some of them said they had fought in seven States, and had never before met our equals. This was putting it on rather thick, but was intended to be in extenuation for their own defeat."

One of Green's cavalry units, presenting a drum captured during the fight to Colonel Roberts's infantry, puffed the victory further: "this battle fought by Texans alone is another warning to the enemy as to what he may expect to suffer should he ever dare to meet the sons of Texas upon their own soil." The *Houston Tri-Weekly Telegraph* added a final insult for General Franklin: "Adoo Yankee General, Adoo, and next time you come, bring along your knitting."

The men in Franklin's army paid no attention to such hyperbole as they marched back toward Vermilionville. They had other problems. Tom Green's persistent horsemen were on their heels again, threatening a grand charge on occasion, withdrawing, darting forward and back, sweeping up stragglers, and generally making life miserable for the unhappy Federals. The Northerners were in no mood now, if they ever had been, to inconvenience themselves for the sake of noncombatant Rebels, and they smashed their way through civilian property much as they had when they had moved in the opposite direction a month earlier. An Iowa soldier could not help but admire the efficiency of his comrades when they decided to construct temporary shelters for themselves: "Two-story dwellings, with outhouses, have been utterly demolished in ten minutes time. While witnessing the performance one could think of nothing but an unfortunate caterpillar, dropped by accident in an ant-bed."

After about ten days in Vermilionville, General Franklin put his army on the road to New Iberia, twenty-five miles to the southeast. Green's cavalry followed closely all the way, observing the Federal columns and striking at isolated individuals and small groups. By the time they approached New Iberia, the Nineteenth Corps had lost about five dozen men to the hovering Confederates. The exasperated commander of the corps finally issued General Order No. 45: "Some few officers and more than 50 men of this command have been taken prisoners by the enemy while outside of the picket lines straggling, stealing, and robbing, going upon unauthorized expeditions or upon expeditions sent by regimental commanders, without authority and without proper escort." To discourage such activity, Franklin ordered that such prisoners be exchanged after all others. Some Federal officers were apparently as disappointed in their men as their soldiers were with them.

On November 17 the blue army finally took up a strong position at New Iberia. General Taylor kept his infantry well away, doubtless realizing the folly of assaulting a much larger foe in prepared earthworks. Instead, Taylor scattered his batteries and foot regiments from Opelousas to the west bank of the Mississippi River while Green's cavalry kept an eye on the Federals.

By early December it was clear that the Texas Overland Expedition was finished. Although he continued to ponder the possibility of a push across south Louisiana (even sending out large cavalry columns to the west), General Franklin kept his army in its works at New Iberia. His divisions never did strike westward across the prairies, and Texas was safe once more from Federal invasion. A few months later, Franklin would lead his corps on the final stab at the Lone Star State, the Red River Campaign. Once again, though, Taylor, Green, and Walker would team to turn back that last thrust.

General Banks's refusal to give Franklin specific instructions about the move toward Texas, Franklin's own timidity, both generals' lack of imaginative solutions to the supply problem, and the stinging defeat on the Bourbeau all spelled failure for the Texas overland campaign.

So, in the end, what did it all mean? What had been accomplished, or lost, in the effort? First, the failure of the Overland Expedition and the feeble success of Banks's landing in far south Texas had diplomatic ramifications. President Lincoln, against the wishes of General Grant, insisted on another push into Texas in the spring of 1864, partly to warn Emperor Louis Napoleon of France away from Texas and the Western Hemisphere.

Second, if the Overland Expedition had succeeded, there would have been no need for the Red River Campaign a few months later. And if there had been no Red River Campaign in 1864, many of the Union divisions sent off on that hapless adventure would have been available for the capture of Mobile and for Sherman's march from Chattanooga to Atlanta and for Grant's drive on Richmond. Who knows what Generals Sherman or Grant might have done with two or three extra corps of tough veterans in their 1864 campaigns? It is certainly possible that they might have finished off the Confederacy sooner than they ultimately did.

Third, Green's cavalry and Walker's infantry demonstrated that trans-Mississippi Confederates, so often overlooked in this war, could take on some of the best veterans in the Union Army in a stand-up fight and live to brag about it—as Texans were inclined to do anyway. Finally, the Lone Star lobby in Washington failed to free Texas slaves and liberate Texas cotton for New England's mills. Similarly, Texas loyalists were prevented once again from establishing a real Unionist government in their home state. Not until the summer of 1865 would the United States Army finally take control of the Lone Star State.

Note: The Table of Organization presented in Appendix A is taken from *War of the Rebellion: Official Records of the Union and Confederate Armies*, Series I, Volume 26, Part 1, Pages 334-336. Republished by The National Historical Society, 1972. The Table of Organization presented in Appendix B is taken principally from the following sources: David C. Edmonds, *Yankee Autumn in Acadiana: A Narrative of the Great Texas Overland Expedition through Southwestern Louisiana, October-December 1863* (Lafayette, LA: Acadiana Press, 1979), Pages 408-409; Norman D. Brown, ed., *Journey to Pleasant Hill: The Civil War Letters of Captain Elijah P. Petty, Walker's Texas Division, CSA* (San Antonio, TX: Institute of Texan Cultures, 1982), Pages 180-181, Note; information from Arthur W. Bergeron, Jr., Baton Rouge, LA, and Donald S. Frazier, Abilene, TX.

APPENDIX A

ORGANIZATION OF FEDERAL FORCES

COMMANDER, DEPARTMENT OF THE GULF
MAJ. GEN. NATHANIEL P. BANKS

COMMANDER IN THE FIELD
MAJ. GEN. WILLIAM B. FRANKLIN

THIRTEENTH ARMY CORPS
MAJ. GEN. CADWALLADER C. WASHBURN

FIRST DIVISION
BRIG. GEN. MICHAEL K. LAWLER

First Brigade
COL. DAVID SHUNK
33d Illinois Infantry, Col. Charles E. Lippincott
99th Illinois Infantry, Col. George W. K. Bailey
8th Indiana Infantry, Lieut. Col. Charles S. Parish
18th Indiana Infantry, Lieut. Col. William S. Charles

Second Brigade
COL. CHARLES L. HARRIS

21st Iowa Infantry, Lieut. Col. Salue G. Van Anda
22d Iowa Infantry, Maj. Ephraim G. White
23d Iowa Infantry, Col. Samuel L. Glasgow
11th Wisconsin Infantry, Maj. Jesse S. Miller

Third Brigade
COL. LIONEL SHELDON

49th Indiana Infantry, Col. James Keigwin
69th Indiana Infantry, Lieut. Col. Oran Perry
7th Kentucky Infantry, Lieut. Col. John Lucas
22d Kentucky Infantry, Lieut. Col. George W. Monroe
16th Ohio Infantry, Maj. Milton Mills
42d Ohio Infantry, Maj. William H. Williams
120th Ohio Infantry, Maj. Willard Slocum

ARTILLERY
1st Indiana Battery, Lieut. Lawrence Jacoby
1st Wisconsin Battery, Lieut. Daniel Webster

THIRD DIVISION
BRIG. GEN. GEORGE F. McGINNIS

First Brigade
BRIG. GEN. ROBERT A. CAMERON

11th Indiana Infantry, Col. Daniel Macauley
24th Indiana Infantry, Col. William T. Spicely
34th Indiana Infantry, Lieut. Col. Robert B. Jones
46th Indiana Infantry, Col. Thomas H. Bringhurst
29th Wisconsin Infantry, Lieut. Col. William A. Greene

Second Brigade
COL. JAMES R. SLACK

47th Indiana Infantry, Lieut. Col. John A. McLaughlin
24th Iowa Infantry, Lieut. Col. John Q. Wilds
28th Iowa Infantry, Col. John Connell
56th Ohio Infantry, Col. William Raynor

ARTILLERY
1ST MISSOURI BATTERY A, LIEUT. CHARLES CALLAHAN

FOURTH DIVISION
BRIG. GEN. STEPHEN G. BURBRIDGE

First Brigade
COL. RICHARD OWEN
60th Indiana Infantry, Capt. Augustus Goelzer
67th Indiana Infantry, Lieut. Col. Theodore E. Buehler
83d Ohio Infantry, Col. Frederick W. Moore
96th Ohio Infantry, Lieut. Col. Albert H. Brown
23d Wisconsin Infantry, Col. Joshua J. Guppey

Second Brigade
COL. WILLIAM J. LANDRAM
77th Illinois Infantry, Col. David P. Grier
97th Illinois Infantry, Lieut. Col. Lewis D. Martin
130th Illinois Infantry, Maj. John B. Reid
19th Kentucky Infantry, Lieut. Col. John Cowan
48th Ohio Infantry, Capt. Joseph W. Lindsey

ARTILLERY
Chicago Mercantile Battery, Capt. P. H. White
17th Ohio Battery, Capt. Charles S. Rice

NINETEENTH ARMY CORPS
MAJ. GEN. WILLIAM B. FRANKLIN

ESCORT
14TH NEW YORK CAVALRY, COMPANY B, CAPT. J. B. AYRES

FIRST DIVISION
BRIG. GEN. GODFREY WEITZEL

First Brigade
COL. GEORGE M. LOVE

30th Massachusetts Infantry, Lieut. Col. William W. Bullock
116th New York Infantry, Maj. John M. Sizer
161st New York Infantry, Lieut. Col. William B. Kinsey
174th New York Infantry, Lieut. William L. Watkins

Third Brigade
COL. ROBERT M. MERRITT

12th Connecticut Infantry, Lieut. Col. Frank H. Peck
75th New York Infantry, Capt. Henry B. Fitch
114th New York Infantry, Col. Samuel R. Per Lee
160th New York Infantry, Lieut. Col. John B. Van Petten
8th Vermont Infantry, Maj. Henry F. Dutton

ARTILLERY
1st Maine Battery, Capt. Albert W. Bradbury
6th Massachusetts Battery, Lieut. Edwin K. Russell

THIRD DIVISION
BRIG. GEN. CUVIER GROVER

First Brigade
COL. LEWIS BENEDICT

110th New York Infantry, Col. Clinton H. Sage
162d New York Infantry, Col. Lewis Benedict
165th New York Infantry, Lieut. Col. Gouverneur Carr
173d New York Infantry, Col. Lewis M. Peck

Second Brigade
BRIG. GEN. JAMES W. MCMILLAN

14th Maine Infantry, Col. Thomas W. Porter
26th Massachusetts Infantry, Col. Alpha B. Farr
8th New Hampshire Infantry, Lieut. Col. George A. Flanders
133d New York Infantry, Col. Leonard D. H. Currie

ARTILLERY
4th Massachusetts Battery, Capt. George G. Trull
1st United States, Battery F, Lieut. Hardman P. Norris

ARTILLERY RESERVE

25th New York Battery, Capt. John A. Grow
1st United States, Battery L, Capt. Henry W. Closson

CAVALRY DIVISION
BRIG. GEN. ALBERT L. LEE

First Brigade
COL. JOHN G. FONDA

1st Louisiana Cavalry, Lieut. Col. Harai Robinson
1st Texas Cavalry, Col. Edmund J. Davis
6th Missouri Cavalry, Maj. Bacon Montgomery
14th New York Cavalry, Lieut. Col. John W. Cropsey
118th Illinois Mounted Infantry, Capt. Arthur W. Marsh

Second Brigade
COL. JOHN J. MUDD

2d Illinois Cavalry, Lieut. Col. Daniel B. Bush Jr.
3d Illinois Cavalry, Capt. Robert H. Carnahan
15th Illinois Cavalry, Company F, Capt. Joseph Adams
36th Illinois Cavalry, Company A, Capt. George A. Willis
1st Indiana Cavalry, Company C, Capt. James L. Carey
4th Indiana Cavalry, Company C, Capt. Andrew P. Gallagher

Not Brigaded

87th Illinois Mounted Infantry, Lieut. Col. John M. Crebs
16th Indiana Mounted Infantry, Col. Thomas J. Lucas
2d Louisiana Mounted Infantry, Col. Charles J. Paine
2d Massachusetts Battery, Capt. Ormand F. Nims

APPENDIX B

ORGANIZATION OF CONFEDERATE FORCES

COMMANDER, DEPARTMENT OF THE TRANS-MISSISSIPPI
LIEUT. GEN. EDMUND KIRBY SMITH

COMMANDER IN THE FIELD
MAJ. GEN. RICHARD TAYLOR

WALKER'S TEXAS DIVISION
MAJ. GEN. JOHN G. WALKER

First Brigade
COL. OVERTON YOUNG

12th Texas Infantry, Col. Benjamin A. Phillpot
18th Texas Infantry, Col. William H. King
22d Texas Infantry, Col. Richard B. Hubbard
13th Texas Cavalry (dismounted), Col. John H. Burnett
Haldeman's Texas Battery, Capt. Horace Haldeman

Second Brigade
COL. HORACE RANDAL

11th Texas Infantry:
    Col. Oran M. Roberts
    Lieut. Col. James H. Jones
14th Texas Infantry, Col. Edward Clark
28th Texas Cavalry (dismounted), Col. Eli H. Baxter
Gould's 6th Texas Cavalry Battalion (dismounted), Maj. R.S. Gould
Daniel's Texas Battery, Lieut. James M. Hamilton

Third Brigade
COL. GEORGE FLOURNOY

15th Texas Infantry (temporarily attached), Col. James E. Harrison
16th Texas Infantry, Col. James E. Shepard
17th Texas Infantry, Col. Robert T. P. Allen
19th Texas Infantry, Col. Richard Waterhouse, Jr.
16th Texas Cavalry (dismounted), Col. William Fitzhugh
Edgar's Texas Battery, Capt. William Edgar

LOUISIANA INFANTRY BRIGADE
BRIG. GEN. ALFRED MOUTON

18th Louisiana Infantry, Col. Leopold L. Armant
24th (Crescent) Louisiana Infantry:
    Col. Abel W. Bosworth
    Lieut. Col. George Soule
28th Louisiana Infantry:
    Col. Henry Gray
    Lieut. Col. William Walker
10th (Yellow Jacket) Louisiana Infantry Battalion, Lieut. Col.
    Gabriel A. Fournet
11th Louisiana Infantry Battalion, Lieut. Col. James H. Beard
12th (Confederate Guards Response) Louisiana Infantry Battalion,
Lieut. Col. Franklin H. Clack
St. Mary's Cannoneers, Capt. Florian O. Cornay
Pelican Artillery, Capt. Thomas A. Faries

GREEN'S CAVALRY DIVISION
BRIG. GEN. THOMAS GREEN

First Brigade
COL. ARTHUR P. BAGBY

2d Louisiana Cavalry (temporarily attached), Col. William Vincent
4th Texas Cavalry, Col. William P. Hardeman
5th Texas Cavalry, Col. Henry McNeill
7th Texas Cavalry, Col. William Steele
13th Texas Cavalry Battalion, Lieut. Col. Edwin Waller Jr.
Valverde Battery, Capt. T.D. Nettles

Second Brigade
COL. JAMES P. MAJOR

1st Texas Partisan Rangers, Col. Walter P. Lane
2d Texas Partisan Rangers, Col. B. Warren Stone
2d Cavalry Regiment (Arizona Brigade), Col. George W. Baylor
3d Cavalry Regiment (Arizona Brigade), Col. George T. Madison
1st Confederate Battery, Capt. Oliver Semmes

FURTHER READING

Arceneaux, William. *Acadian General: Alfred Mouton and the Civil War.* 2d ed. Lafayette, LA: Center for Louisiana Studies, 1981.

Bartlett, Napier. *Military Record of Louisiana.* Baton Rouge: Louisiana State University Press, 1964. Reprint of 1875 edition.

Beecher, Harris H. *Record of the 114th Regiment, N.Y.S.V.: Where it Went, What it Saw, and What it Did.* Norwich, NY: J. F. Hubbard, Jr., 1866.

Bentley, William H. *History of the 77th Illinois Volunteer Infantry.* Peoria, IL: Edward Hine, 1883.

Bergeron, Arthur W., Jr. *Guide to Louisiana Confederate Military Units, 1861–1865.* Baton Rouge: Louisiana State University Press, 1989.

Blessington, Joseph Palmer. *The Campaigns of Walker's Texas Division.* Introduction by Norman D. Brown and T. Michael Parrish. Austin, TX: State House Press, 1994. Reprint of 1875 edition.

Bringhurst, Thomas H., and Frank Swigart. *History of the Forty-Sixth Regiment Indiana Volunteer Infantry.* Indianapolis: Regimental Association, 1888.

Cade, Edward W. *A Texas Surgeon in the C.S.A.* Edited by John Q. Anderson. Tuscaloosa, AL: Confederate Publishing Co., 1957.

Clark, Orton S. *The One Hundred and Sixteenth Regiment of New York State Volunteers.* Buffalo, NY: Matthews and Warren, 1868.

Connor, Orange Cicero, and Mary America Connor. *Dear America: Some Letters of Orange Cicero and Mary America (Aikin) Connor.* Edited by Seymour V. Connor. Austin, TX: Jenkins Publishers, 1971.

Edmonds, David C., ed. *Official Report Relative to the Conduct of Federal Troops in Western Louisiana, During the Invasions of 1863 and 1864, Compiled from Sworn Testimony, under Direction of Governor Henry W. Allen.* Lafayette, LA: Acadiana Press, 1988. Reprint of 1865 edition.

_____. *Yankee Autumn in Acadiana: A Narrative of the Great Texas Overland Expedition Through Southwestern Louisiana, October–December 1863.* Lafayette, LA: Acadiana Press, 1979.

Fitzhugh, Lester N., comp. *Texas Batteries, Battalions, Regiments, Commanders, and Field Officers, Confederate States Army, 1861–1865.* Midlothian, TX: Mirror Press, 1959.

Harrington, Fred Harvey. *Fighting Politician: Major General N.P. Banks.* Philadelphia: University of Pennsylvania Press, 1948.

Hendrickson, Kenneth E., Jr. *The Chief Executives of Texas: From Stephen F. Austin to John B. Connally, Jr..* College Station: Texas A&M University Press, 1995.

Hoffman, Wickham. *Camp, Court and Siege: A Narrative of Personal Adventure and Observation during Two Wars.* New York: Harper & Brothers, 1877.

Hosmer, James K. *The Color-Guard: Being a Corporal's Notes of Military Service in the Nineteenth Army Corps.* Boston: Walker, Wise, and Co., 1864.

Irwin, Richard B. History of the Nineteenth Army Corps. New York: G. P. Putnam's Sons, 1892.

Jackson, Isaac. *"Some of the Boys...": The Civil War Letters of Isaac Jackson, 1862–1865.* Edited by Joseph Orville Jackson. Carbondale: Southern Illinois University Press, 1960.

Kerby, Robert L. *Kirby Smith's Confederacy: The Trans-Mississippi South, 1863–1865.* New York: Columbia University Press, 1972.

Lane, Walter P. *The Adventures and Recollections of General Walter P. Lane*. Marshall, TX: News Messenger Publishing Co., 1928.

McGregor, Frank Ross. *Dearest Susie: A Civil War Infantryman's Letters to His Sweetheart*. Edited by Carl E. Hatch. New York: Exposition Press, 1971.

Marshall, Albert O. *Army Life: From a Soldier's Journal*. Joliet, IL: Chicago Legal News Co., 1884.

Marshall, T.B. *History of the Eighty-Third Ohio Volunteer Infantry: The Greyhound Regiment*. Cincinnati: Eighty-Third Ohio Volunteer Infantry Association, 1912.

Noel, Theophilus. *Autobiography and Reminiscences of Theophilus Noel*. Chicago: Theo. Noel Co., 1904.

Oates, Stephen B. *Confederate Cavalry West of the River*. Austin: University of Texas Press, 1961.

Parks, Joseph H. *General Edmund Kirby Smith, C.S.A.* Baton Rouge: Louisiana State University Press, 1954.

Parrish, T. Michael. *Richard Taylor: Soldier Prince of Dixie*. Chapel Hill: University of North Carolina Press, 1992.

Petty, Elijah P. *Journey to Pleasant Hill: The Civil War Letters of Captain Elijah P. Petty, Walker's Texas Division, C.S.A.* Edited by Norman D. Brown. San Antonio: University of Texas Institute of Texan Cultures, 1982.

Scott, Reuben B. *The History of the 67th Regiment Indiana Infantry Volunteers*. Bedford, IN: Herald Book and Job Print, 1892.

Stanyan, John M. *A History of the Eighth Regiment of New Hampshire Volunteers*. Concord, NH: Ira C. Evans, Printer, 1892.

Stevenson, B. F. *Letters from the Army*. Cincinnati, OH: W.E. Dibble & Co., 1884.

Stuart, A.A. *Iowa Colonels and Regiments: Being a History of Iowa Regiments in the War of the Rebellion*. Des Moines, IA: Mills & Co., 1865.

Sutton, Aaron T. *Prisoner of the Rebels in Texas: The Civil War Narrative of Aaron T. Sutton, Corporal, 83rd Ohio Volunteer Infantry.* Edited by David G. Maclean. Decatur, IN: American Books, 1978.

Taylor, Richard. *Destruction and Reconstruction: Personal Experiences of the Late War.* Introduction by T. Michael Parrish. New York: Da Capo Press, 1995. Reprint of the 1879 edition.

Voorhis, Aurelius Lyman. *The Life and Times of Aurelius Lyman Voorhis.* Edited by Jerry Voorhis, Sr. New York: Vantage Press, 1976.

Whitcomb, Caroline E. *History of the Second Massachusetts Battery (Nims' Battery) of Light Artillery, 1861–1865.* Concord, NH: Rumford Press, 1912.

Wiley, Bell Irvin., ed. *This Infernal War: The Confederate Letters of Sgt. Edwin H. Fay.* Austin: University of Texas Press, 1959.

Winters, John D. *The Civil War in Louisiana.* Baton Rouge: Louisiana State University Press, 1963.

Woods, J.T. *Services of the Ninety-Sixth Ohio Volunteers.* Toledo, OH: Blade Printing and Paper Co., 1874

PHOTO CREDITS

We acknowledge the cooperation of the United States Army Military History Institute at Carlisle Barracks, Pennsylvania, for the photographs of Nathaniel P. Banks, Stephen G. Burbridge, Edmund J. Davis, William B. Franklin, Andrew J. Hamilton, Albert L. Lee, William Marland, James R. Slack, Edmund Kirby Smith, Richard Taylor, and Cadwallader C. Washburn.

We are grateful to the Harold B. Simpson Confederate Research Center, Hillsboro, Texas, for providing photographs of Arthur P. Bagby, Richard Coke, James P. Major, Oran M. Roberts, and John G. Walker.

For the photograph of Thomas Green we credit the Archives Division, Texas State Library, Austin, Texas.

The following pictures were reproduced as they appeared in *Leslie's Illustrated Weekly*: Federal troops crossing Vermilion Bayou; the Battle of Buzzard's Prairie; St. Landry Catholic Church; the attack on the 60th Indiana; the Opelousas Courthouse.

The picture of a Federal soldier shooting an alligator was reproduced as it appeared in *Harper's Weekly*.

The picture of the capture of the 67th Indiana is attributed to Corporal Rueben Scott in his *History of the 67th Regiment*.

The picture of William Marland's charge across Bayou Bourbeau was reproduced as it appears in David C. Edmonds' *Yankee Autumn in Acadiana* (The Acadiana Press, Lafayette, Louisiana, 1979).

INDEX

Abbeville, La., 44
Abolitionists, 14
Alabama, University of, 72
Alexandria, La., 25, 26, 39, 44
Algiers, La., 34
Alligators, 41, 42-43
Andrew, John A., 15
Atchafalaya River, La., 26, 34
Atkinson, Edward, 15

Bagby, Arthur P., 78, 88; photograph of, 77; *see also* Texas
    cavalry
Banks, Nathaniel P., 17, 59, 110; photograph of, 18; sketch of,
    20-21; as commander of Texas Overland Expedition, 25, 36;
    and Brownsville expedition, 61-62
Barre's Landing, La., 58, 60, 61, 63
Bayou Boeuf, 72, 80
Bayou Bourbeau, 13, 53, 56, 65, 68, 73
Bayou Teche, La., 25, 26, 36, 39, 41
Berwick City, La., 36
Blair, Montgomery, 15
Brashear City, La., 26, 34, 35, 36, 46
Brownsville, Tex., 47
Buehler, Theodore, 88, 93
Burbridge, Stephen Gano, 66, 68, 74, 75, 107;
    photograph of, 67; at Battle of Bayou Bourbeau, 82-85, 88
Butler, Benjamin F., 16
Buzzard's Prairie, La., 53-56, 65, 99

Cajuns, 13, 25, 26, 39
Carrion Crow Bayou, 65, 68, 83, 98-99
Casualties, at Battle of Bayou Bourbeau, 103-4
Centerville, La., 41

Chretien Point Plantation, 53, 57
Clark, Edward, 59
Coke, Richard, 59, 84; photograph of, 84
Confederate artillery: 1st Regular (Semmes's) Battery, 53, 55
Congressional Medal of Honor, 95
Corsicana, Tex., 82
Cotton, 14, 15, 20, 26, 47

Daniel, James M., 73
Davis, Edmund J., 59 photograph of, 33; as cavalry
    commander, 33-34, 47, 55, 63
Davis, Jefferson, 27
Department of the Gulf (Federal), 17, 31

Fonda, John G., 68, 74-75, 83, 96
France, 20, 22, 26, 47, 110
Franklin, William B.: at Sabine Pass, 22; photograph of, 23;
    commander of Nineteenth Army Corps, 31; commander of
    Overland Expedition, 39, 53, 60-61, 63; retreats, 65, 105,
    109-10; on defeat, 107

Galveston, Tex., 19, 22, 26
Grand Coteau, La., 75, 79
Grant, Ulysses S., 20, 66, 110
Green, Thomas, 39, 49, 61, 75, 100, 107; sketch of, 29;
    photograph of, 50
Guppey, Joshua, 82, 88-89, 107

Halleck, Henry W., 19, 20, 21
Hamilton, Andrew Jackson: photograph of, 16; sketch of, 17;
    as Unionist governor, 19, 22
Houston, Sam, 59
Houston, Tex., 22, 26
Hubbard, Richard B., 59

Indiana Infantry: *60th,* 65, 83-85, 86-88, 104; *67th,* 41, 65, 79, 82, 83, 85, 88-93, 103-4

Jackson, Thomas J. "Stonewall," 20-21, 28
Juarez, Benito, 20

Kansas, 32
Kentucky, 66

Lee, Albert L.: photograph of, 32; as cavalry commander, 32-34, 59
Lee, Robert E., 19
Lincoln, Abraham, 93; and Texas, 15, 17, 110

Magruder, John B., 19
Major, James P.: photograph of, 76; *see also* Texas cavalry
Marland, William, 95; photograph of, 94
Massachusetts artillery: 2nd (Nims's) Battery, 54-55, 68, 83, 95
Matamoros, Mex., 47
McClellan, George B., 16, 19
Mexico, 17, 20, 22, 47
Milliken's Bend, La., 29
Mississippi River, 17, 19, 20, 26
Monroe Doctrine, 20
Mouton, Jean Jacques Alfred Alexander, 29, 39

New Iberia, La., 44, 60, 61-62, 109-10
New Orleans, La., 17, 19, 22, 25, 34
New Orleans, Opelousas and Great Western Railroad, 34-35
New York infantry: *114th,* 57
Niblett's Bluff, La., 26, 44, 45, 48, 60, 61
Nims's Battery, *see* Massachusetts artillery
Nineteenth Army Corps (Federal), 31, 63; rivalry with Thirteenth Army Corps, 36-39; destruction by, 40, 41, 57; at Buzzard's Prairie, 53-54; retreats, 65, 109; on defeat, 107

Ohio artillery: 17th Battery, 67, 75, 83

Ohio infantry: *83rd*, 66, 79, 83, 88, 93; *96th*, 66, 74, 83-85, 88, 92, 94, 102, 104

Opelousas, La., 56, 60, 72, 73; Federal occupation of, 58, 60, 61, 70-71; after Battle of Bayou Bourbeau, 100-2, 104

Ord, E.O.C., 56

Owen, Richard, 66

Port Hudson, La., 19, 20, 25, 26, 31

Red River, 19, 20, 21, 25, 45

Roberts, Oran M.: as governor, 59; photograph of, 69; as infantry commander, 69, 73, 75, 78; sketch of, 72; at Battle of Bayou Bourbeau, 80, 85, 96

Sabine Pass, Tex., 22

Sayers, Joseph, 53, 59

Semmes, Oliver, 53

Semmes's Battery, *see* Confederate artillery

Sherman, William T., 66, 110

Shreveport, La., 19, 20, 48

Slack, James R., 99; photograph of, 98

Smith, Edmund Kirby, 45; photograph of, 44; strategy of, 59

Stanton, Edwin, 17

Taylor, Richard, 39, 41, 50, 58, 107; photograph of, 27; sketch of, 27-28; strategy of, 59-60, 61, 65, 109-10

Texas: and slavery, 14, 15; and secession, 15; as target of invasion, 15-16, 17, 19, 20, 22, 25, 26; Unionists in, 17, 19, 35, 47, 111

Texas artillery: Valverde Battery, 53-54, 73, 89; Daniel's Lamar Artillery, 73

Texas cavalry, 29, 47, 49, 57, 68, 107, 109-11; *1st* (U.S.), 33, 49, 63; *16th* (dismounted), 65; Major's brigade, 76, 89, 99, 103; Bagby's brigade, 78, 89, 103

Texas governors, 59
Texas infantry, 108, 111; *11th*, 72, 78-79, 84, 88, 96; *14th*, 59;
    15th, 59, 72, 78-79, 82, 84, 101, 104; *17th*, 45, 58, 64;
    18th, 72, 78-79, 84, 88-89; *22nd*, 59
Textile industry, 14, 15, 16-17, 20, 22
Thirteenth Army Corps (Federal), 31, 63, 108; rivalry with
    Nineteenth Army Corps, 36-39; destruction by, 40, 41,
    56-57; at Buzzard's Prairie, 56; retreats, 65; at Battle of
    Bayou Bourbeau, 99; on defeat, 105, 107
Trans-Mississippi Department (Confederate), 19, 20, 45

Valverde Battery, *see* Texas artillery
Vermilionville, La., 44, 46-47, 48, 49, 60; destruction in, 56, 109
Vicksburg, 19, 20, 26, 31, 66

Walker, John G., 64, 103, 108; photograph of, 28; sketch of, 29
Walker's Texas Division, 29, 45, 57, 64, 72, 73, 111
Washburn, Cadwallader C., 59, 99, 105; photograph of, 30;
    sketch of, 31
Washington, La., 58-59, 64, 72
Wisconsin infantry: *23d*, 66, 75, 79, 82, 83-85, 88, 96